KU-504-114

A SIGNIFICANT OTHER

RIDING THE CENTENARY TOUR DE FRANCE
WITH LANCE ARMSTRONG

Matt Rendell

PHOENIX

A PHOENIX PAPERBACK

First published in Great Britain in 2004
by Weidenfeld & Nicolson
This paperback edition published in 2005
by Phoenix,
an imprint of Orion Books Ltd,
Orion House, 5 Upper St Martin's Lane,
London WC2H 9EA

10 9 8 7 6 5 4 3 2 1

Copyright © 2004 Matt Rendell

The right of Matt Rendell to be identified as the author of
this work has been asserted by him in accordance with the
Copyright, Designs and Patents Act 1988.

All rights reserved. No part of this publication may be
reproduced, stored in a retrieval system, or transmitted, in
any form or by any means, electronic, mechanical,
photocopying, recording or otherwise, without the prior
permission of the copyright owner.

A CIP catalogue record for this book
is available from the British Library.

ISBN 0 75381 874 4

Printed and bound in Great Britain by
Clays Ltd, St Ives plc

www.orionbooks.co.uk

'In 2003 Lance Armstrong won his fifth Tour de France in its centenary year. But Matt Rendell's gripping retelling of this most contested and dramatic stage race is really the story of Armstrong's heroically loyal *domestique*, the Colombian, Victor Hugo Peña, and an essential insider's overview of the whole event. Both Peña and Rendell are the perfect companions, articulate, open-hearted and passionate. *A Significant Other* is a tour de force of endeavour, landscape, history, and – something rare in the world of sport though central to the world of cycling – altruistic generosity'

Jim Crace

'A superb piece of work . . . Victor Hugo makes a superb subject – he seems very articulate and a gifted storyteller in his own right . . . and the intercut chapters about the history of the Tour are beautifully written and remarkably fresh in content and insight'

Matt Seaton

'Rendell elegantly elucidates the tactical technicalities of cycling's unique mixture of co-operation and competition, teamwork and individualism . . . Through Peña's transcribed first-person accounts, Rendell places us right in the midst of the swarming bunch'

Guardian

'. . . there is a scholarly quality to *A Significant Other*, a short but powerful book that uses the diary of a *domestique* in the 2003 Tour de France as the counterpoint to the author's exploration of the true nature of top-class competitive cycling . . . you won't find a better analysis of the extraordinary collective feat that is a team of cyclists working together at speed'

Independent on Sunday

'A rare sports book that actually gives an idea of the experience of being a professional athlete'   *TLS*

'Matt Rendell's book is a cultured addition to the genre . . . Rendell is exquisitely alert to the race's higher significance'   *Independent*

'Rendell packs in a great deal of very useful information, while that unforgettable day is recaptured vividly'
Daily Mail

Matt Rendell survived Hodgkin's Disease and lecturing at British and Latvian universities before entering TV and print journalism. His first book *King of the Mountains: How Colombia's Cycling Heroes Changed their Nation's History* (Aurum Press 2002) was described in *The Times* as 'meticulous, elegant and sensitive'. His Channel 4 documentary about sport in Colombia and Ecuador, also called *Kings of the Mountains*, was described in the *Observer* as 'a gem, telling us more about the essence of sport in under an hour than a season's worth of Premiership matches'. He has written for the BBC, ITV and Channel 4, including British coverage of the Tour de France, and he edited *The Tour de France Centennial 1903–2003* (Weidenfeld & Nicolson 2003). The National Sporting Club named Matt Rendell 'Best New Sports Writer 2003'.

In Memoriam
Augusto Triana, Nestor Mora, Hernán Patiño

Contents

All photographs courtesy of Offside Sports Photography apart from Victor Hugo Pēna aged 10 and and Hugo Pēna Moreno which are both courtesy of Victor Hugo Pēna.

... le vélo, c'est de la voile.

Cyrille Guimard, La folie du Tour

And I sometimes wonder if I ever came back, from that voyage. For if I see myself putting to sea, and the long hours without landfall, I do not see the return...

Samuel Beckett, Molloy

But as a rule the ancient myths are not found to yield a simple and consistent story, so that nobody need wonder if details of my recension cannot be reconciled with those given by every poet and historian.

Diodorus Siculus, Bibliotheca historica Book IV, 44: 5, 6

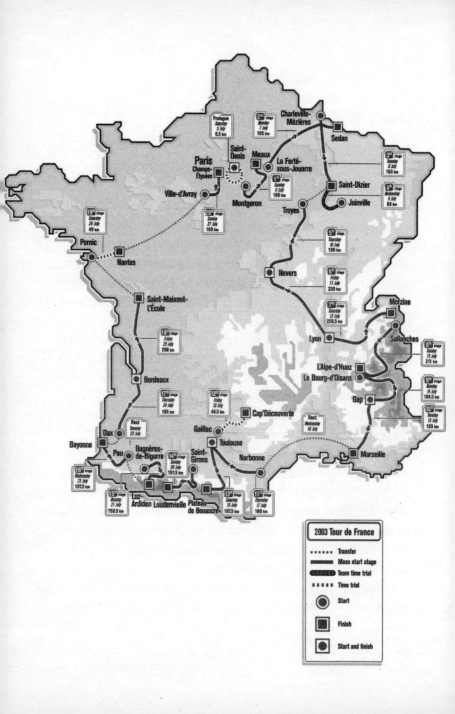

Prologue
Saturday
5 July
6.5 km

2nd stage
Monday
7 July
195 km

Charleville-
Mézières

Sedan

Saint-
Denis

Meaux

La Ferté-
sous-Jouarre

3rd stage
Tuesday
8 July
160 km

Paris
Champs-
Élysées

Ville-d'Avray

Montgeron

1st stage
Sunday
6 July
160 km

Saint-Dizier

Joinville

4th stage
Wednesday
9 July
69 km

19th stage
Sunday
26 July
49 km

20th stage
Sunday
27 July
160 km

Troyes

Pornic

Nantes

Saint-Maixent-
L'École

Nevers

5th stage
Thursday
10 July
196 km

6th stage
Friday
11 July
230 km

Morzine

7th stage
Saturday
12 July
226.5 km

Sallanches

Lyon

8th stage
Sunday
13 July
211 km

18th stage
Friday
25 July
200 km

Bordeaux

L'Alpe-d'Huez
Le Bourg-d'Oisans

9th stage
Monday
14 July
184.5 km

Gap

10th stage
Tuesday
15 July
195 km

17th stage
Thursday
24 July
165 km

12th stage
Friday
18 July
48.5 km

Cap'Découverte

Rest
Tuesday
22 July

Dax

Gaillac

Toulouse

Marseille

Bayonne

Pau

Bagnères-
de-Bigorre

Saint-
Girons

Narbonne

Rest
Wednesday
16 July

16th stage
Wednesday
23 July
197.5 km

15th stage
Monday
21 July
159.5 km

Luz-
Ardiden Loudenvielle Plateau
de Bonascre

14th stage
Sunday
20 July
191.5 km

13th stage
Saturday
19 July
197.5 km

11th stage
Thursday
17 July
160 km

2003 Tour de France

······· Transfer

——— Mass start stage

▨▨▨▨ Team time trial

▪▪▪▪▪ Time trial

◉ Start

▣ Finish

◉ Start and finish

Preface

The heat was oppressive for seventeen days. The sky to the south was smothered by billows of smoke over forests of fire-stripped trees. Everything was hazy and depleted. Elsewhere, there were storms. Cattle and cars were swept across the flood plains by murderous tides. It was as if, incited by the duel below, the gods themselves had taken up arms against each other. For a central rivalry lies at the heart of every great sporting challenge. Player and Nicklaus, Senna and Prost, Ovett and Coe: each was both mirror and lens, reflecting and magnifying the other until both assumed the stature of giants. The history of cycling, too, is a history of inspiring rivalries: Bartali and Coppi, Anquetil and Poulidor, Merckx and Ocaña, Hinault and Lemond. In 2003, Lance Armstrong and Jan Ullrich proved theirs worthy of the tradition. Armstrong gained time in the team time trial and on Alpe d'Huez. Ullrich thrashed him over the Cap' Découverte time trial, then stole back more seconds on the Plateau de Bonascre.

Yet as the titans stalk each other, opportunities appear for others: Palmer, Mansell and Cram were also great champions; so too Koblet, Gaul, Gimondi and Fignon. And as Armstrong and Ullrich traded blows, the Kazakh Alexander Vinokourov outrode them both on stage eight to Alpe d'Huez, again on the following day's stage into Gap, and once more on stage fourteen through the Pyrenees to Loudenvielle. After sixty-one hours in the saddle spread over fifteen days of racing, just eighteen seconds separated them – eighteen seconds, when, after hours of exertions, a tired rider on a steep gradient can lose two minutes per kilometre on his rivals! Three players on deuce in the final set; three teams separated by goal difference before the final day of the season. Never had it been so close. What an appropriate way to celebrate the Tour a hundred years on – by tightening the tension until the wire was ready to snap! This book tells the story of stage fifteen of the 2003 Tour: a stage into which the universe of the Tour de France – the universe of cycling itself – lay latent, ready to reveal its secrets.

A hundred and ninety-eight riders started the Tour; just a hundred and fifty-four started the stage, a sprawling mountain odyssey from the spa town of Bagnères-de-Bigorre in the shadow of the Pyrenees, north into a horseshoe over the Lannemezan moors, south beside the Aure river, upward and westward over the great mountain pass over the Col d'Aspin and the towering Tourmalet, down to the village of Luz-Saint-Sauveur, then up fifteen writhing kilometres to the finish line at the ski resort of Luz-Ardiden. Many were swaddled in bandages where the skin had been scraped clean off the muscle, or bound in tape to splint broken fingers or relieve fractures in the upper body. Some were nearing physical breakdown, and would not last the day. The Italian team sponsored by the cement manufacturer Fassa Bortolo had been reduced to three riders by infections of the upper respiratory tract, a characteristic hazard as the remorseless pace eats away at the immune system. Joseba Beloki, the most aggressive of Armstrong's opponents in the early mountain stages, slipped on a road surface liquefied in the heat of stage eight. The impact left him with breaks to the trochanter in the right femur, and with the ulna and radius in the right arm protruding through an open wound. David Etxebarria, on the Basque Country team Euskaltel-Euskadi, was so ill during the long time trial that he stopped to vomit. The jury of commissaires then slapped a two-minute, five-second penalty on Etxebarria for slipstreaming behind another rider, taking his total time beyond the permitted limit. Etxebarria was duly expelled from the race.

The Tour offers no compassion. If the lungs and legs are still intact, there is no giving up: this is the code of the Tour de France. This brutality encloses the riders in a community of toil, the numb mystery of cycling. Perhaps that is why, of all sporting events, the Tour de France is the most acutely conscious of its own history. Its routes are studies in self-quotation and metered by monuments to the dead, and every act of victory or defeat opens a dialogue with the past. The first Tour de France was held in 1903; of the annual global sporting events that can claim such antiquity, neither the five English classic flat races that started with the St Leger in 1776, nor the British and US Open golf tournaments (1860 and 1895 respectively), nor even Wimbledon (1877) can match it in duration or in the many nations that comprise its field. And the Tour was not merely a tournament for an established sport, but an entirely novel invention: a *stage* race, where before there had only been one-day races, and a *national* stage race at that. By comparison, the Olympics (1896) were a revival, not a new idea, while the America's Cup (1870) and the Ashes (1880) have the same imaginative spark, but are occasional challenges with neither the continuity nor the multinational ethos of the Tour. Few events, ancient or modern, are built on such a broad foundation of relentless self-sacrifice.

Two-thirds of the way through the Centenary Tour de France, only five of the twenty-two teams taking part still had their full complement of riders; the US Postal Service team was one of them. Lance Armstrong was in the yellow jersey. Three Spaniards opened the road for him into the mountains: José Luis Rubiera, known as 'Chechu'; Manolo Beltrán, or 'Triki'; and Roberto Heras. In the foothills, two Americans tunnelled through the air: Floyd Landis and George Hincapie; and on the long, flat stretches, Russia's Viatcheslav Ekimov, the Czech rider Pavel Padrnos, and Colombia's Victor Hugo Peña sped ahead of the group, leading the champion in their wake.

An Ocean of Air

Cycling is an anomaly of modern sport and has often confounded the unfamiliar. Neither properly individual nor strictly for teams, it sits awkwardly on the gaps between the normal categories. It imports aerospace and Formula One technology, only to make physical demands that drive body and mind to breaking point. It measures performance to the thousandth of a second, then lumps a hundred athletes or more into the same time as they swarm across the line. It obliges most of its players to renounce personal ambition for a tiny handful of leaders – worker ants or drones, selflessly committed to serving their sovereign – yet disposes them in global rankings based on individual results. A strange half-breed of a sport, then, from whose awkward obscurity looms a poker-faced figure with an athlete's nervous tension and a long list of household chores: the *domestique*. Whenever his leader punctures or needs a toilet stop, someone must be on hand to pilot him back to the front or, in an emergency, give him a wheel, two, or the entire bike. Someone, too, must coast back to the team car with discarded clothing or helmets, or to fill their shirt with as many water bottles as the seams will resist, and battle to the front with the extra weight to keep their team-mates hydrated – demeaning tasks for men mislaid in an identity parade of identically dressed peers. Behind dark glasses and a helmet, shuffled into the pack, the domestique can expect little recognition from the public, and less from the press; the constraints on media time and space mean his efforts are either effaced by the delete key or forgotten in the rushes. He has other errands to run: joining long-distance breakaways, for instance, but without taking his turn at the front; or, if he is well placed in the classification, sacrificing all in decoy attacks to draw out the vigour of his leader's in-form rivals. But these are all secondary tasks. The domes-tique's *raison d'être* is to transfer energy from his muscles into the surrounding atmosphere – to tunnel through the still air and create a moving stream in his wake. In normal life, the petty turbulence that fills the spaces we vacate, the insig-nificant by-product of lives spent scurrying like sea insects over the floor of an atmospheric ocean of air, melts incon-sequentially. Cycling adopts it as a founding principle, exer-cising the minds of scientists for whom the sport is essentially a venerable experiment in applied fluid mechanics.

The scientists, of course, convert athletic duress into the abstract currency of power units; what matters is not the exchange rate but the relative loads of the parties concerned. One study finds that a rider at the head of a single file sus-taining sixty kilometres per hour must generate 607 watts of power – an output the fittest amateur could manage for no more than a matter of seconds. Diving into the comet's tail of chasing air, the rider in second position has only to produce seventy-one per cent of the first rider's work rate to maintain the same speed. Carried along by these two, riders three, four and the rest can keep up on just sixty-four per cent of the first rider's graft. If, instead of exploiting his work, the remaining three cooperate with him and all four take equal turns pulling at the front and recovering behind, they will each save a quarter of the energy a lone rider would consume at the same speed – and will collectively be able to maintain the blistering pace far longer. So powerful is the effect that the following rider feels as if he is being towed: cyclists even call their turn at the front a 'pull'. Pulling at the front is the physical basis of teamwork in cycling – a line of domestiques sharing the load ahead of their leader – but it is also the principle behind the attack and the chase, for when a single rider or a small group breaks away from the pack, their only hope of building a lead is to work together. The more riders taking turns at the front, the greater the energy saved; however well organised, a small group cannot normally match the speed of a long, organised draft line involving many riders. This is the paradox at the heart of cycling: to compete, even rivals must cooperate. In doing so, the play of accommodation and opposition creates complex systems never quite in equilibrium, yet rarely chaotic for long, oscillating around limits defined by shared interest.

At stage races like the Tour de France, the team time trial turns this mathematical complexity into a choreographed and highly visual art as nine team members take carefully cali-brated turns at the front. Teams set off at five-minute intervals, allowing their members to keep the benefit of their wake among themselves; it's the one true team stage of the Tour. In the mass-start stages, slipstreams are shared between riders of all teams, and drafting gives rise to more complex forms. Biding their time before the decisive attack, the favour-ites shelter behind their domestiques, who pour energy into their protective slipstream until they have no energy left. The team leaders ride as economically as possible until the critical moments – the ones where the race is won and lost; the ones that make the highlights packages and the sports pages. By the time the broadcast has started and the press room has begun to fill, successive waves of domestiques have already often fallen off the pace and been dropped into public oblivion, to finish the day five, ten, twenty minutes back, or in the safety net of the *gruppetto*, riding *tempo* on a theoretical fold at the back of the stage, nurturing no greater ambition than that of gaining the finish within the allowed time. Half an hour or more behind the stage winner and the overall contenders, the *gruppetto* mothers home the exhausted, the injured, the sick – and the fakers, storing away energy for a future attack, knowing the *gruppetto*'s the place: at high speeds, surrounded by a large group in a moving stream of air, an individual rider's work rate plunges dramatically. One rider in the scientific literature, with great concentration, bike-handling and drafting skills, rode a six-hour Tour de France stage at an average speed of forty kilometres per hour and an average power output of just ninety-eight watts – a figure within reach of the most leisurely village priest. In the most favourable possible conditions, with no wind, level roads and a fastidious aerodynamic tuck, a solo rider would have to produce two and three-quarter times more power to maintain such a speed, leaving the country curate trailing. Nor is riding in a tightly packed peloton for the faint-hearted. Elbows and shoulders touch; rising rear wheel arcs float just ahead of descending front wheel arcs in a tantalising design fault that causes regular and bloody falls. The pack is electrified with nervous energy. Touch the brakes, however imperceptibly, and you'll plummet from the back of the group – and there are worse scenarios.

The protected riders who benefit from their domestiques' attentions are athletes of proven abilities – an aristocracy of talent, not inherited privilege. The use they make of their domestiques depends on the race situation. For the race leader, one constellation of domestiques shares the load until the mountains; another cluster negotiates the foothills; and a final pair will shepherd the leader up the epic ascents. Those off duty at any time shuttle between the race lead and the team vehicle 500 metres behind, carrying water to keep their colleagues hydrated. The race leader's main rivals will exploit his slipstream with just a couple of domestiques on hand; the rest will be under orders to regain the strength to create mayhem another day. When a winning margin has been opened, the leader's domestiques will guide him home as his rivals burn themselves out in futile pyrotechnics: the team secures the individual's triumph.

Which is where the discrepancy emerges, for cycling is one of those modern mythologies that celebrate solitary talent. The domestique's very existence threatens to undermine the very greatness of the greats. Would Ali be such an icon if he'd merely won some early rounds, then cowered behind a bodyguard for the rest of the bout? Would Jesse Owens, if he'd taken over just to dip for the line? The principle is not restricted to sport. Isn't a painting by Raphael's workshop justly less valuable than the work of the artist's own hand? Suppose Paganini had sent an understudy to perform the concerto, and the maestro had burst from the wings only for the final cadenza: there would have been a riot! Children may dream of delivering the match-winning assist in other sports; there isn't one who dreams of becoming a domestique. A water carrier, the insult goes, and the phrase is the domestique's alias. Not the champion's equal. Not even a runner-up. With respect to the contenders, the domestique is the Other: perhaps not even *the* Other – *an*other, at most, lost in the crowd, but significant all the same, one of a team of significant others who lurk at their leader's shoulder like Siamese twins – like Siamese nonuplets – concealed in an overcoat. Unfit to fight for greater glory, the domestique travels steerage where, unwelcome on the upper deck and with no lifeboat place reserved, he is destined to sink beneath the waves of memory with the rest of history's surplus. Unsurprisingly, he has no counterpart elsewhere in sport. American football has its offensive linemen and soccer its midfield stoppers, but they are their team-mates' equals in victory or defeat. Great yachts-men and mountaineers have support climbers and crew, but when their expeditions are done, the hierarchy dissolves. Even the journeyman boxer can land the sucker punch. If there is a parallel, it is from the stage-managed cruelty of the bullfight: the anonymous picador who goads and weakens the bull before the matador's acclaimed execution. When the killer moment comes, after sometimes hundreds of kilometres of probing, softening up, accumulating physical and mental fatigue, the leader seizes the strategic second to surge through his domestiques' protective envelope and open an advantage so wide, a wall of still air can descend behind him. It is his sole mission, and his ability to perform it again and again against the best opposition gives him his special status. For leading him loyally to that moment, day after day and in race after race, the domestique receives a wage that may be substantial, but is often less. A lesser wage for a lesser athlete, perhaps a lesser man, for assuming the lesser role?

Ours is an age obsessed not just with success, but with stories of success. One of the most compelling is Lance Arm-strong's, the tale of a prodigiously talented, prodigiously ambitious Texan kid who stared mortality in the eye and turned the cancer that was killing him into the fuel of inspiration. His remarkable life has resonated beyond his sport – beyond sport *tout court* – and out into a wider society hungry for miracles. That he is a cyclist, as opposed to a marathon runner or a musician, is beside the point. The success story transcends the local circumstances that produced it. The domestique is different. However well he performs his duties, his success will be equivocal; he cannot transcend the world that sustains him, or meet worldly standards of gratification. Instead, he embodies the uncertainties encoded in the very structure of cycling – human, social, even philosophical questions about the division of labour, the limits of altruism and the extent to which even the most fortunate of lives must fail to realise its potential for happiness. If Don Delillo is right, and 'longing on a large scale is what makes history', it may be worth listening to his story, for cycling is certainly one of humanity's great spectator activities. Each July, the Tour de France eclipses virtually every other sports event worldwide, claiming a global television audience of two billion, plus fifteen million roadside spectators. In May and September, the Tours of Italy and Spain galvanise their homelands. Elsewhere, cycling brings sport and a spirit of celebration to people all around the globe. Stage races in Venezuela, Australia, Malaysia and Qatar open the international calendar: competitions in Kazakhstan, Curaçao, New Zealand, Japan, Costa Rica and Honduras close it. In between, races in Africa, the Baltic States, Brazil, Canada, Chile, China, Colombia, the United States, and all over Europe, East and West, draw enormous crowds and prove cycling's cross-cultural appeal – this, despite closing roads, laying siege to towns and bringing disruption wherever it passes. If cycling's emotional yield outweighs the local inconvenience it causes – and in all but the Anglo-Saxon countries, it seems to – it is perhaps that the cyclists bring some secret psychic fulfilment to the ranks of their beholders.

I first met Victor Hugo Peña one chill Milan morning in March 2000, before the start of the famous one-day race to San Remo. We had spoken several times by telephone; in the flesh, he was as warm, charismatic and ambitious.

'I'd just turned twenty and I was riding the national tour for riders aged twenty-two and under, a week-long race. On only the first stage, two hard mountain climbs shook out the weak, and on the hardest ascent there were only fifteen riders left in the leading group; I was one of them. We were catapulting into the descent when my team leader broke hard ahead of me, feet stretched out to either side to avoid a fall. He had punctured. I stop, whip open the brake calliper, flick the quick-release lever and pass him my front wheel. Seconds later, he hurls himself after the leaders. I stand at the side of the road with a castrated bike in my hand as the entire field goes by. The road's so narrow, I have to wait for everyone to pass before my team car can reach me and give me another wheel. I lose ten, fifteen minutes, but at the end of the week, my team leader is the winner. By giving him my wheel, I've helped him win, and one day, my turn will come. The following year, I was a domestique again. The year after that I was injured, which meant I'd lost my chance. Then they introduced the Under-23 category, and gave me another year. And this time, I won.'

Victory at last in the 1996 Under-23 Tour of Colombia was a major step in Victor Hugo Peña's progress towards pro-fessional cycling. He'd been travelling to compete in Europe since 1996; I'd been visiting Colombia since 1998. At the time of my first visit, Victor Hugo was in northern Spain, riding strongly in the five-day Euskal Bizicleta and the four-day Trofeo Castilla y León. There, he caught the attention of Javier Mínguez, the manager of a major Spanish team sponsored by Vitalicio Seguros, a firm owned by the Italian insurance giant Generali Assicurazioni. In the colours of Vitalicio Seguros, Victor Hugo left the isolated gene pool of Colombian national cycling and became an international player. At the Tour of Italy in May and June 2000 we spoke almost every day. The day before the first long time trial, Victor Hugo told me he thought he could win. I met up with him the morning after he had. That victory, over a mirror-flat route through the north-east Italian region of Friuli, transformed him from a little-known South American into a respected and feared time-trial specialist. But Victor Hugo could do more than ride flat stages against the clock. He was also an excellent climber, one of an elite group of young riders seemingly beckoned by greatness.

However, in spring 2000, his team sponsor issued a curt press statement announcing their withdrawal from cycling sponsorship. It read: 'Vitalicio Seguros entered cycling sponsorship for the purposes of publicity. The team's successes contributed to increased brand awareness from 37.9 per cent in March 1997 to 53.8 per cent in March 2000.' The harsh economic reality occupied by cycling teams, who draw their funding from the publicity departments of great corporations, closed its jaws around the staff and riders of the Vitalicio Seguros cycling team.

'After the Giro I had a high market value. I signed a pre-contract binding me to a major Italian team, but the contract fell through at the end of the summer, when my market value had already dropped. There were offers, but for less than half what I'd agreed in June. During the Tour of Burgos in northern Spain, I said to my agent, "Why not talk to Bruyneel?" [Johan Bruyneel, the Belgian polyglot and former rider who master-minds the US Postal Service team]. He left the hotel, then called me and said, "Have you got a moment?" I said, "What for?" "Bruyneel wants to talk." I left the hotel immediately. Bruyneel told me to clear up whatever I had with the agent, because whatever Bruyneel had to say to me wasn't going to change. He showed me a list of riders who were in his plans for the next year. I was one of them. "If you'd like to come, I'd like to have you." I said, "Of course." The money he had to offer was practically the same as I'd been offered in June. He said, "I haven't got a contract to give you straight away, but I'll give you my hand, which I think is sufficient, if you believe in a man's word." I said, "Yes, you should know that my hand is also worthy."'

That winter, investigating the mysteries of Colombian cycling, I visited Victor Hugo in his homeland. He welcomed me like an old friend. With his father Hugo and his brother Ismael, we talked about everything, but mostly cycling. We went riding together, Victor Hugo conversing easily, me suf-fering beside him as silently as I could. He introduced me to ex-cyclists in the town of Bucaramanga, neighbouring Victor Hugo's beloved Piedecuesta – literally, 'foot of the climb'. And we talked about the excitement of joining the cycling team of the US Postal Service, and flying up to Texas to meet Lance Armstrong. The greatness for which Victor Hugo once seemed destined has never quite happened, although today, he *is* a multiple Tour de France champion, the winner of every Tour de France he has entered. Won, as in ridden on the winning team – although his team has never won the team competition.

His team is Lance Armstrong's team, and Victor Hugo is one of Armstrong's domestiques.

Suppose a talented young athlete of your acquaintance joined the New York Yankees or Real Madrid or became a Ferrari test driver, or started training beside Wayne Gretsky, Michael Jordan or Pelé. You'd glow with pride. The US Postal Service team is cycling's greatest team and Armstrong its genius. That handshake with Johan Bruyneel bound Victor Hugo's future to theirs. Yet when he joined the US Postal Service cycling team in autumn 2000, I was almost disappointed. Besides Armstrong, the finest rider of his generation, US Postal meant Roberto Heras, the remarkable Spanish climber, and Viatcheslav Ekimov, the great Russian who had just defeated Armstrong to win the Olympic time-trial title. My friend would be moving from a position of relative freedom into the rigorous discipline of the professional domestique, with the undercurrent of ambiguity that goes with it. I was a little sorry for myself, too: every sportswriter wants to be able to look back and say, 'I knew Merckx before he was great'; no one looks wistfully back on their first encounter with a water carrier. But perhaps we should. If greatness has so far eluded Victor Hugo – as it eludes most of us – he has been given an excellent vantage point on one of the finest, most driven athletes in world sport, and through his own slipstream he has contributed organically to his success. If cycling speaks through the domestique, it must do so through Victor Hugo – even during his leader's most memorable *individual* performances, including, perhaps, the greatest stage of the closest Tour in a hundred years.

21 July 2003: Bagnères-de-Bigorre, Pyrénées-Atlantiques. The water here is water and rock. Over the forest land of the Bigorre, early mists condense on the foliage and the droplets start a long limestone seepage. The slow penetration enriches them with calcite and aragonite which, far below and into the future, they will deposit into an underground world glistening with gypsum and white lilac. Where the bedrock approaches the surface, the watercourses spill into resurgent springs. In ancient times, animals must have traced instinctive lines across the landscape connecting nest, feeding ground and natural well. Perhaps nomadic humanity tracked goats, deer and wild pigs along these trails, treading them into primitive paths. After their camps had become permanent settlements, those intuitive tracks were metalled and mapped. The past of the ancients is buried in asphalt now. Modernity has its own histories. Today, other teams of hunters will follow the ancient paths into the mountains.

General Classification after stage 14
Total distance: 2485 km
Leader's time: 61 hrs 7 mins 17 secs
Leader's average speed: 40.655 kph

1	ARMSTRONG Lance	US Postal-Berry Floor	1	USA	
2	ULLRICH Jan	Team Bianchi	131	GER	15 secs
3	VINOKOUROV Alexander	Team Telekom	28	KAZ	18 secs
4	ZUBELDIA Haimar	Euskaltel-Euskadi	179	ESP	4 mins 16 secs
5	MAYO Iban	Euskaltel-Euskadi	171	ESP	4 mins 37 secs
6	BASSO Ivan	Fassa Bortolo	81	ITA	7 mins 01 secs
7	HAMILTON Tyler	Team CSC	71	USA	7 mins 32 secs
8	MANCEBO Francisco	iBanesto.com	31	ESP	10 mins 9 secs
9	MOREAU Christophe	Crédit Agricole	121	FRA	10 mins 9 secs
10	SASTRE Carlos	Team CSC	78	ESP	12 mins 40 secs
97	PEÑA Victor Hugo	US Postal-Berry Floor	8	COL	2 hrs 11 mins 5 secs

Beginnings

Monday 21 July 2003, 07:30: Mercure Palais des Sports, Pau. Victor Hugo Peña

My eyes snap open. I don't remember where the door is, or the bathroom. A muddled question coalesces in my head: is this yesterday's hotel or today's? I spend twenty nights of the season at the flat in Spain. The rest is spent in hotels. They mystify the memory. I find I can remember a hotel, but I can't relate it to a place. I know we stayed at tomorrow's hotel last year, but not today's. The hotel after the stage, yes, but not the one before. I sometimes wake up in my flat in Spain, thinking it's another hotel, and when I'm in Colombia, I open my eyes the first morning and can't believe I'm home after so many nights spent in temporary surroundings.

Unless we have a very early start, I don't use an alarm clock. In the rhythm of the Tour, my eyes open at seven-thirty. When I was new to it, I used to get so tired I couldn't sleep. I'd lie there, knowing I wouldn't be able to recover without sleeping, and the worry would make it worse. But I've learned how to centre myself on the race, and sleeping has become a professional skill. You ride like a professional, and you learn to sleep like one. If I've fallen or had some sort of physical problem in the race, it may repeat itself in my head, over and over again. Occasionally, I'll dream I'm in the peloton, trying to accelerate away but unable to. But normally I sleep well. I eat dinner and go straight to bed. I don't leave the hotel. At most, I read, listen to music, or watch TV. If I'm writing, I write in bed with my legs up. If I'm reading, I read in bed with my legs up. I spend all my free time in bed. Cyclists are like the chronically ill: we rest insatiably. You need every moment of recovery you can get.

Each night we're given a printout saying what time we have to be up, what time we have to hand in our luggage, what time breakfast starts, what time we leave the hotel. Today, breakfast is at eight-fifteen, and the atmosphere is tense. There's an air of expectation. Someone says, 'I can't do this any more . . .' But you need to be able to eat in the morning, to eat spaghetti and rice for breakfast after two weeks of eating spaghetti and rice for breakfast. Pasta, cereal, rice with fried eggs, coffee, bread, Nutella. It's just another part of the job. Eat like a professional; force it down. It isn't a good time for humour; say something frivolous, and it might not come across that way. So no one speaks. Everyone keeps himself to himself. It's the most nervous breakfast of my life. I don't want to say anything to him or pass him anything. Or rather, I want to, but I hold back. I think he knows the silence is centred on him. It may be creating even more pressure. He's probably thinking, 'I'm responsible for this. I'm the guilty one.'

Because we share rooms with each other, we know each other as well as married couples. I know how my team-mates sleep. I'm sharing with Pavel Padrnos. He doesn't care whether the light's on or the TV's on. He's already asleep. Ekimov reads religiously during the Tour, after dinner. Last year I shared a room with him, and the final evening, he slammed the book shut ceremonially and announced: 'Five!' Chechu's diligent with his stretching routine. And he uses every last second of sleep he can get. He comes down to the table at the last possible moment, and we laugh when he arrives because he's always last. Roberto talks in his sleep, although I'm not telling you what he says because what I know about them they know about me. They know what I sound like when I'm speaking to my girlfriend, and that I say 'Si, señor' or 'Si, señora' to my parents or to older people. They ask me, 'Why do you say "Si, señor" to your father?' They're amazed we're still so formal in Colombia.

I've shared with Lance, too. Most Americans are messy; you go into an American's room and there are things all over the floor. Lance is different. He's neat, methodical, systematic. Nothing's out of place. His room looks like the boss's room. And he never seems tired. He's like a clock; he knows what he has to do with every moment of his time, he deals with whatever has to be dealt with. Just watching him is an education. It's not just how he rides, it's how calm he is. He doesn't expend nervous energy. And he never says, 'I can't do this, it hurts too much.' He fights to the bitter end. That's his way of riding: fearless. That's what you learn during the races. Then, there's the training. Early in the season, you're at a race, and with two days to go before it ends, he says, 'Johan, have you booked the mechanic's ticket to St Moritz in three days?' 'Don't worry, it's all taken care of.' We're in the middle of a race and he's already thinking about training at St Moritz in three days. And when he says: 'Today, four hours,' he trains for four hours. If it's, 'Today, six hours,' it's six. Even if he can't breathe. If tomorrow is five hours and the following day is two, it's five and two, not two and five or three and four. The afternoon after you train with him, your knees ache, you can't walk. You think to yourself: 'How am I going to do four and a half more hours of this tomorrow?' No one trains like him. And in the morning, he's the first to the breakfast table. If breakfast's at nine, he's there at eight-thirty. The first time I trained with him in the US, we rode for eight hours. And that was in January, months before we start racing. In other teams, it's the *directeur sportif* or the team doctor who says, 'Let's go! Time to train.' In this team, it's Armstrong. He says, 'Breakfast at eight?' And the masseur or whoever has to prepare breakfast says, 'OK, I'll have the table ready for ten to eight.' The following day, he comes down, half asleep, and there's Armstrong. He's been there since seven-thirty, drinking coffee, reading the newspaper. It's a bit of a shock to see the boss already there, waiting for you. You have to get up early with Armstrong.

When he's feeling good, he's the sort of guy who says so. Over the past few days, when the press ask us how he is, we've always given the same answer: 'Better than ever. Completely recovered. As good as last year.' But we say it without knowing the truth. He and Ullrich have both had problems. Lance's began in June: at the Dauphiné Libéré, he fell at nearly 80 kph, and had to have chiropractic treatment. The week before the Tour began, he suffered gastroenteritis. On stage one of the Tour, he was caught in a mass fall, and his chiropractor flew in again. On stage eight, he climbed the entire Galibier with the front brake rubbing the rim. Ullrich was also ill that day. During the Cap' Découverte time trial, Lance became severely dehydrated. On Bonascre, both of them were ill: Lance was still suffering the after-effects of dehydration; Ullrich had diarrheoa and had to stop at the roadside. He smelled of shit all day, and his team-mates poured water on him to clean him up.

Now, I don't know how Lance is. He keeps saying, 'I think I'm OK. I believe I'm OK.' We aren't used to it. I can't remember a day in the past when he wasn't ... The silence makes me think: perhaps he's nervous or afraid, or just concentrating. I don't really know what he's thinking. But I'm feeling OK, thank God. My body is tired, but I know every other rider at the Tour feels the same. And unlike other teams, our training is focused on the Tour. In any case, if we were on any other team, any one of us could be in the top ten. So if everyone's tired, so much the better. We're the champion's team, he's wearing the yellow jersey, and we're ready for a fight. Perhaps that's the reason behind the silence. Rudy Pevenage, Jan Ullrich's confidant, has been to the coach to ask for a yellow jersey signed by Lance. Someone in the team has promised to get one for him, but there's always something to do, and it's been forgotten. When Lance was drinking coffee on the team bus this morning, the *soigneur* told him, 'Rudy said, "Don't bother. We'll have one of our own soon enough." '

At the team meeting, Johan gives us the day's plans. There's a twenty-second bonus on offer for the stage winner at Luz-Ardiden. Lance leads Jan Ullrich by fifteen seconds; to widen his lead to more than a minute, he needs that bonus. So if Lance is on form, we need to deliver him safely to a position from which he can launch a stage-winning attack. That means no big escapes can be allowed to get away. We have to keep any breakaway small, and within ten minutes, so that it can be brought back towards the end of the stage. Ekimov, Padrnos and I are responsible for the first eighty kilometres. If a breakaway gets away, either George or Landis has to be in it. The first hour is the most dangerous, Johan tells us; we have to be ready to suffer for the first hour of the stage. On the day we climbed the Lauteret – the Lauteret and the Izoard:

the stage to Gap – five of us were stuck in the chasing group after only twenty kilometres. The stage started fast, everyone was going hard, and we had to chase down so many attacks that eventually five of us – Landis, Ekimov, Padrnos, Rubiera and me – were recovering at the same time. When the next acceleration came, we could do nothing about it. Lance, George, Roberto and Triki were in the front group, and the five of us were in a group behind them. They couldn't slow down, because the attacks persisted, so we pulled the chasing group along for fifteen kilometres, half a minute behind them, without gaining any ground. At moments like that you think, *If the five of us can't get back in touch, the four of them will have to ride 180 kilometres, and they won't all be with Lance at the end.* We caught up with them eventually, I don't know how; maybe we were just stronger than everyone else.

It's humid at the stage start, but the heat has eased. Rain seemed to threaten, but the threat has dispersed. We're there half an hour early. In any other job, no one arrives at the office half an hour early. In cycling, it serves a purpose. There are 198 riders at the Tour, which means 198 names in dozens of languages. We need to be able to recognise them all, identify their strengths and weaknesses, know when they've been saving energy in the *gruppetto*, what part of which stages will suit them, when they're strong and when they're weak. We don't know each other well, but we have a functional familiarity. The peloton is like a huge, open-plan office with 198 employees working together. The difference is, we all sign in at the start of the day, and get the chance to mix before the working day begins. Then, on the road, the clerks change desks every few minutes and work beside different colleagues, then divide into committees of ten or fifteen or twenty for longer periods each day. We get to know more of our workmates than most professions – not well, but well enough to know we form part of a small community, sharing the same lives, the same goals, the same tragedies.

Lauri Aus, a sprinter from Estonia, was killed two days ago. He was crushed to death by a truck with a drunk driver. All I knew about him was his name, and that he was part of our small community. With Andrei Kivilev, it was different. We knew each other well enough to greet each other at races. During the Tour of Valencia in February, his team was in a hotel thirty kilometres from my flat. The race started with an afternoon time trial, so in the morning I went out to train and met him coming the opposite way. He raised his hand and smiled. The image will probably remain with me for ever. He died two weeks later, after falling head first at Paris–Nice. Afterwards I read he grew up high in the mountains far from the races in Europe. Like me. When I was a child, a lorry ran into a group of riders during the Tour of the Táchira in Venezuela, killing a friend of my father, Manuel Cárdenas, and two other riders. He raced for Café de Colombia and was the first rider I knew who had a car. I can still remember it: a Fiat Mirafiori. My parents and I wept. Then, when I was on a training ride with the Postobón team in Colombia, a lorry came around a corner and ran into us. Three team-mates – Augusto Triana, Nestor Mora and Hernán Patiño – were killed. I still miss their company, their friendship, their laughter. After Kivilev died, I thought of his wife and child, and Vinokourov. Kivilev was his best friend, and he was close to Aus too. We stand behind the starting line in silence. Aus's team-mates on AG2R Prévoyance wear black ribbons of remembrance. There are tears on their faces. They will want to commemorate him with a stage win. But they'll have to win on merit. The Tour hangs on today's stage.

Then, we're waved off. This isn't the start of racing; this is a ceremonial start to let the host town see the riders. We weave slowly through the streets of Bagnères-de-Bigorre to a second starting line where the racing begins. Before we get there, Lance lets the entire peloton pass until the team car reaches him. He may have a radio problem; they never work at the stage start because there are so many of them. Roberto and Chechu go with him. I have to be near the front with Pavel. The Tour de France is a complex spider's web of races within races: the race for overall victory, the top ten places and the title of best young rider; the race for the overall points and mountains categories; the race to be the best team; and the race to win the day. Every day there are riders who go out to win the stage. If they can't get away, they go back to the *gruppetto* to recover. They don't care about finishing in the top twenty overall, or whatever. They're the ones who'll make our life hard today. We both know there's going to be war. I'm not tired any more: I'm feeling prepared. This is the day I've been waiting for. I have the whole structure of the stage in my head. There are a couple of climbs in about thirty kilometres. I know what's coming.

At the foot of a shallow incline in the outskirts of Bagnères-de-Bigorre, we reach the real stage start. A sudden acceleration shudders through the peloton. I can see Massimiliano Lelli, a powerful Italian in the red, white and blue colours of the Cofidis team, stringing out the peloton along the left-hand margin of the road as it rises. Yesterday's stage winner, Gilberto Simoni, in bright red, veers out of his slipstream across to the right. The only rider with him is the Dutchman Michael Boogerd, who shoots past Simoni in a flash of orange and leads him away. They quickly have fifty metres. Beneath a screaming harmonic, the air pulses to the beat of helicopters overhead. We're still in suburban Bagnères-de-Bigorre, yet the speed already has several riders in distress.

One, I know well. As we take the bend, I can see Iván Parra clinging to the back of the peloton. He was violently ill a couple of nights ago, and hasn't recovered. We live near each other in Spain, and rode together for Vitalicio Seguros. When I was a kid, playing with my best friend, we'd pretend we were our favourite cyclists, and I'd always be Iván's brother, Fabio. I don't know why we changed our names, and the game could be football or anything, not cycling, but he'd be Lucho Herrera and I'd be Fabio Parra. Lucho was the greatest climber in the world, and finished fifth, sixth and seventh in the Tour de France. Fabio was an all-rounder and finished third in the 1988 Tour. They were the pride of Colombia. When I first heard about Iván, he was a road cyclist and I was a swimmer. Then, when I started racing on the road, he'd become a mountain-biker. I only ever saw him from a distance. I'd see him training and someone would say, 'Look, that's Fabio's brother.' Halfway through 1995, he joined Manzana Postobón, the team I was riding for. We weren't friends. I'd helped our team leader, Bernardo Pedraza, win the 1993 Youth Tour. On the hardest climb of stage one, I was in the leading group with only fifteen others. As we began the narrow descent, Bernardo punctured and I gave him my wheel. After the race my father said, 'The wheel you gave Bernardo won him the Tour. If you want to be a cyclist, you'll have to get used to the idea.'

Nineteen ninety-four was my second year with the team, and I worked for another rider who won the Youth Tour, Freddy Moncada. The following year was to be my turn. I knew I could win the time trials, hang on uphill, and manage the team. Then Iván joined and the rivalry began. Every time he said he was going to win the Youth Tour, I thought, 'Join the queue.' Then, a month before the Tour, I suffered a knee injury. It kept me out for six months, and Iván won it. Then they created the Under-23 category, giving me another chance the next year. This time Iván was injured and I won the Tour. From then on, he took his path and I took mine, until we met at Vitalicio. At home in Colombia, we'd been the best. In Europe, we discovered a much harder form of cycling, and gave each other mutual support. We ended up close friends. He finished ninth in the 1999 Tour of Spain, when he was only twenty-four. He would have finished in the top ten of the 2000 Tour of Italy if he hadn't broken his wrist. Then he moved to ONCE, where he was out of favour and lost two years of his career. Now he's riding for Kelme, trying to retrieve the time he lost. But the Tour is unforgiving, and Iván will have no top ten finish this year.

Ahead of me, Simoni has been unable to stay close to Boogerd, and drops away. It's hardly surprising: while Simoni was winning yesterday's stage, Boogerd was putting his feet up; he finished in a *gruppetto* of forty-four riders, thirty-two minutes and fifty-six seconds behind Simoni. We still haven't ridden three kilometres, yet the speed is already very high. Motorbikes zoom past, slowing and surging ahead of us as the cameramen and photographers frame and angle their images. Rounds of thin applause and shouts reach us from small clusters of spectators as we hurtle past. There are occasional calls from the riders, mostly warnings. Boogerd has been caught by a green-clad Kelme rider, Javier Pascual Llorente, riding fast at the front. The peloton is stretched out in single file; at least two gaps have opened in the line. The Cofidis rider David Moncoutié assumes the first position. Now Boogerd relieves him. Now it's José Azevedo, the only Portuguese rider on the Tour, dressed in the pink uniform of the

ONCE-Eroski team. He powers away from them and opens a small advantage. Even a short climb would enhance gravity's weight in the equation of forces that oppose us, loosening the slipstream effect and giving him a chance of extending his lead. But there is no climb. Azevedo knows that, alone, this outlay of energy is pointless, and relents. The Spaniard David Cañada takes over, and he too gains a short lead. Then the same thing happens: no climb comes, and he eases back into the group. Boogerd takes over the frontal position again.

As we approach the village of Orignac, six kilometres into the stage, the road rises slightly. A rider in the red of Brioches la Boulangères eases past Boogerd: it is Sylvain Chavanel, one of the best young French riders. He finished with the *gruppetto* yesterday, perhaps thinking of today. He has a Spaniard, Pablo Lastras, on his wheel. They share the work, opening a lead of thirty metres. The other attackers – Boogerd, Azevedo, but also Paolo Bettini, the best one-day rider in the world, and Jörg Jaksche, seventeenth overall, accelerate to close the gap. Bettini came in at nineteen minutes and forty seconds. Jaksche, riding for a team with no leader since Beloki's fall, worked hard yesterday. In their shelter, I accelerate too.

We leave the village and the landscape opens. Speeding along a rolling country lane, Pavel takes over the load-bearing position at the front of the race. I roll past him, and from this point, we'll work as a single mechanism. Three riders flash past my right shoulder: Moncoutié and Chavanel, with the former champion of Italy Salvatore Commesso between them. I accelerate violently to close them down. Chavanel persists, opening a small gap until the shortest rider in the Tour, Samuel Dumoulin of the Jean Delatour team, attacks, leading us past Chavanel and opening a short gap himself. But as the rest of the US Postal team moves towards the front, Dumoulin comes back. We have ridden seven kilometres. The next time Dumoulin attacks, he steers a group of four into a small lead. Two riders are trying to reach them across the gap, metres ahead of the peloton. I'm sixth from the front of the main field, with Pavel just behind. Azevedo is among the four at the front. He's far more powerful than the other three, and when he moves into the lead, a small gap opens. They have to work hard to stay in his slipstream. Without meaning to, Azevedo is helping me control the race by wearing down the other attackers. The riders ahead of me are determined to be in the breakaway when it forms. I draft in their wake, letting them neutralise each new attack. The peloton now forms one continuous line, moving very fast.

As each attack flares out into the space ahead of the group, the riders in it glance over their shoulder at us. They want to see if we'll react and suck them back in, or release them. Last year, Laurent Jalabert – one of the most exciting riders of the 1990s and a French hero – rode up to me and I said, 'Go.' 'You'll let me go?' 'We'll let you go.' Jalabert was the king, the breakaway hero. But he needed our permission to go. There were times when so many riders tried to follow that we had to chase them down. It ruined Jalabert's attacks, but we couldn't let twenty go. There's no frisson of triumph when you go past a failed group of breakaway riders. I try not to look at them; I don't want to seem arrogant. I've often been in their situation, wanting to break away but not being allowed to, so I don't feel superior. In a Tirreno-Adriatrico I rode, I remember Bettini coming past and laughing. Since then, even if I only want to see who's around me, I try not to look at them.

There's a lot of communication between us on the radio. Whoever has a clear view informs the others – 'Boogerd's attacking,' or whatever. We ask Johan who's at the front, and he tells us what Radio Tour tells him. If you have a breakaway of twenty, all on different teams, with a dangerous rider in it, no one is going to want to help us. The hardest days for the domestiques defending the yellow jersey are days like this, when a large group of riders attack. There can be fifteen of them, and one of them may be just five minutes off Lance in the classification. That means eight of us against fifteen of them. In theory, the team of the rider in third place reacts first, because he doesn't want to lose his position. Then it's the team of the second-placed rider. Then it's us, the leader's team, and suddenly there's an alliance, twenty-four against fifteen. But the second- and third-placed riders are also competing with the race leader, and any alliance has to endure mind games and kidology. So we're constantly receiving updates. On days like this, when it's important to catch the breakaway, the first thing Johan says is, 'No CSC, no Cofidis,' so we know which teams will be interested in cooperating. Chavanel is persisting. As we go through Luc, he has opened a small gap. Pavel's behind me. We keep the pace high, but we don't try and chase everyone down. The stocky Commesso leads four more riders, with two chasers just behind them, and another four riders just ahead of me. We hold them there. George Hincapie is with them. Then we start a small climb. A gap appears in the line of riders ahead of me, and a breakaway forms. I try to close the breach, but Lance says, 'Easy, easy,' knowing George is there. I'm just behind George, on a curve, when Lance says, 'Let them go,' and we ease back.

George is speaking into his radio, saying who's in the break. We have to be able to process the rush of information pouring into our ear. Azevedo, Botero, Chavanel, Commesso, Glomser, Pascual Llorente and Bettini – all strong riders, as is the Belgian Mario Aerts; there is a Basque, Iñigo Landaluze, and a strong Russian in Alexander Bocharov. The rest are French and could work together. They are Nicholas Vogondy, last year's champion of France; Benoît Poilvet, Christophe Oriol and Andy Flickinger, all of whom I had a good look at during the Dauphiné Libéré in June; and Nicolas Portal, who is always on the attack. Flickinger, Oriol, Portal and Bocharov are all team-mates on AG2R Prévoyance. Only Glomser, Pascual Llorente and Bocharov finished within nineteen minutes of Simoni yesterday, so most of these riders should have energy to burn today. I finished in the group with Aerts and Poilvet, nearly half an hour after Simoni. But they'd been recovering all day. I'd ridden a hundred kilometres at the front.

Santiago Botero, the only other Colombian at the Tour, is leading. He finished in a group of fourteen riders yesterday, all timed at twenty-six minutes and twenty-nine seconds. His Tour has been ruined by sickness. I've known him since 1994. I saw him at the Clásica de Antioquia, a regional stage race in Colombia. He was twenty-two, and it was his first road race, riding for a team sponsored by the sports doctor who had discovered him. The stage from the town of Caucasia to Yarumal has a fifty-seven-kilometre climb, and everyone was looking on with great expectation. Botero was a university rider who'd started as a weekend mountain biker, then won the Clásico *El Colombiano*, a mass event for the general public, in a time so fast they thought there was something wrong with the clock. No one knew who he was, in a sport where everyone usually knows everyone. Ten kilometres up that huge climb, I heard the radio in the car that was accompanying me say Santiago was in the leading group of twenty or thirty. I was in the second half of the field, and I caught up with him in a village called Puerto Valdivia. He turned to me and asked, 'How much further is there to climb?' I pointed to a sign that said, 'Valdivia 21 km.' He's always been the same – the same ingenuousness, the same soft personality – almost too soft to be winner. At times, he respects his rivals too much; he knows he can win, but he respects who he's going to beat. Everyone looks at him and knows how strong he is; the only one who doesn't know it is Santiago. There are times when he's the hot favourite, and he denies everything before running away with it. I reached Yarumal that day with two good climbers, Hernán Buenahora and Olmedo Carpacho. I was in my room, getting washed, when Santiago finished. He was ill, and I don't think he started the following day. I saw him again when he was part of the Postobón track team, riding the individual pursuit for Colombia.

In 1997 we were both riding for Kelme. We had a training camp in Medellín, Santiago's home town, and we went out time-trial training, riding ten-kilometre repetitions, one leading, the other on his wheel. I rode my ten, then Santiago roared past and I couldn't even get into his slipstream. His power is incredible. The following day we went out on a four-hour ride. When we got back he said, 'I'm going out for another hour or so.' I went in, showered, had lunch, waited, and waited, and he arrived two hours later. Now he's the reigning world time trial champion. I've never really ridden head to head against him, although I'd like to. I beat him in the Prologue of the Tour. At the first long time trial, he was ill and I was under team orders not to race. In the final time trial of the 2002 Tour, he was eighth and I was tenth. I'd love to ride against him and have two Colombians competing for the world championship.

Three CSC riders and four Cofidis move ahead of me to lead the chase, in what we call the Ball formation – a double line, in which you pull until you reach the front, then peel off, like convection bubbles in boiling water. The breakaway is simmering in the same pattern, like a mirage before us, until Bettini sits up. He has probably already been told that CSC and Cofidis are chasing, and knows that the attack isn't going to get away, so he'll sit at the back and watch, saving energy, working only when the others notice and tell him to. Normally you see who's in the break and know if the breakaway is going to get away. If it isn't, you don't go to the front because you know it's a waste of energy.

We jolt across a level crossing after nineteen and a half kilometres. The computer on my handlebars tells me that the average speed so far is fast: 47.5 kilometres per hour. There are still 140 kilometres to go, including six climbs: three are fourth category, one is first category and two are *hors caté-gorie* giants. Lance is behind Landis and Ekimov, about twenty-five riders back from the head of the peloton. The breakaway has a seventeen-second lead. It's my moment to demonstrate that I'm ready for war. We are now riding at seventy kilometres per hour. Not many riders can impose this type of speed. Some can't keep up even in your slipstream. It's not a speed you can maintain for long. The fact that I know I'm on the best team, part of the team of the leader of the Tour, fills me with strength. The harder they attack, the more we want to show that they have to deal with us. It's a battle, and the strongest will win. If they want to go fast, we want to go faster, and make it harder still. Whoever wants to win is going to have to go over us.

After twenty-six kilometres, we reach the foot of the first major climb of the day, the fourth-category Côte de Meilhas. The gradient shatters the leading group. Three riders break away from the peloton to try to get across to the breakaway group. I look around and realise I'm at the head of a group of riders that has become detached from the main field containing Lance. I reach George, who says, 'Wait for everyone to arrive.' Behind me, Pavel is at the front of the peloton. Meanwhile, the breakaway has split and Bettini is working again, knowing it might get away. Only Chavanel, Botero and George can stay with Bettini. Then Chavanel accelerates powerfully, pulling away alone. I see Botero respond, before they disappear. They have a fifty-metre lead over a chasing AG2R rider and a small group. Botero overtakes Chavanel, and they begin to work together. At the back of the peloton, riders are being dropped. Three minutes after making their attack, Botero and Chavanel are caught by a new breakaway group. I'm some way behind, but I can see Boogerd and the green jersey of Baden Cooke, who's thinking of the intermediate sprint in eight kilometres. In his desire to get away, Boogerd has been labouring at the front for much of the stage, punching the first tunnel through the air for the rest to follow. But he won't get far. In the balance of favours given and accepted, Boogerd has a bad debt. At the 2002 Amstel Gold Race, the most important one-day race in Holland, Boogerd, a Dutchman on a Dutch team, asked Lance to help him win, promising Rabobank's help at the 2002 Tour. Lance fulfilled his part of the bargain, but Boogerd was beaten in the sprint by two stronger riders. At the Tour, Johan called in the favour, not because we needed it, but as a point of principle. Rabobank refused. Lance ended his friendship with Boogerd, and at the 2003 Amstel Gold, said something like, 'Anyone but him.' So, it's unlikely Boogerd will be allowed to get away, even if he has the strength.

It is just past one o'clock. We have ridden twenty-nine kilometres when I catch the remains of the breakaway on the hill. Just three riders remain ahead of us: Botero, Chavanel and Patrice Halgand, the leader of the Jean Delatour team.

Armstrong tells me to let them go. We release them from our gravitational pull: now, we want them to pull away. We want them to go to stop the accelerations and allow us to set our own pace – as long as they're visible they'll attract others who want to join them. Instead, they hang there before us. They cross the top of the climb just six seconds ahead. We've covered thirty-one kilometres in forty minutes, an average of 46.5 kilometres per hour. I'm leading, Pavel is behind me, with Eki in third place. From here to the mountains, the three of us will work as a single organism. Lance is on Eki's wheel. The peloton is so strung out it will take twenty-five seconds to pass.

Chavanel dives into the descent, with Botero close by. Pavel leads the peloton. On the Côte de Bugard, Halgand loses contact with Chavanel and Botero. A group of six riders, with one just behind, try to get off the front. I hold them just ahead of me, before gently pulling them back. We emerge out of a wood to see Halgand ten seconds ahead of us. Botero and Chavanel are half a minute up the road. At one-fifteen and ten seconds, we pass Halgand. It has taken us forty kilometres to impose our authority on the stage. We have allowed just two riders to escape and established the shape of the race for the immediate future. Johan told us our first job of the day would take an hour. We've done it in fifty minutes.

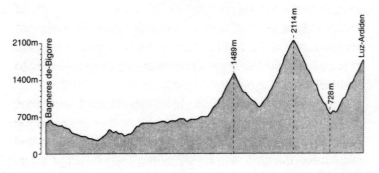

Order from Chaos

The stage is fifty minutes old. Bruyneel's first wave of domestiques – Peña, Padrnos and Ekimov, with Hincapie monitoring the breakaway – has won an important battle. They have even earned a five-minute respite by allowing the attack a small lead and inducing CSC and Cofidis to set the extreme pace of the pursuit. There may be more attacks ahead, but the riders tempted to join them now know they'll be resisted. The pattern for the next eighty kilometres has been set. Yet, that a pattern can emerge at all where we might expect a dogfight, is worth remarking. For although the essence of the Tour is austere in its simplicity – the fastest rider to the finish wins – the detail glistens with design.

The most important table of standings is the general classification, or GC (without the determining article). GC decides overall victory, the best young rider and the team competition, and has been decided by overall time for most of the Tour's history, although a points system was tried from 1905 to 1912. Today, official timings have some of the feel of an abstract points system, for, despite the astonishing accuracy of electronic chronometry, they are ultimately the product of human judgement. A gap between mechanical and official timings is opened by the time deductions awarded to the first three across each intermediate sprint and stage finish. Deductions of various magnitudes have been used since the 1920s: without them, André Leducq would have won the 1932 Tour by three seconds, not twenty-four minutes and three seconds. In 2003, time bonuses in all three three-week Tours were standardised at six, four and two seconds for the first three in each intermediate sprint, and twenty, twelve and eight seconds for the first three in the stage. The rule allotting the same time to riders who finish together – a measure introduced to discourage dangerous manoeuvres in the final straight – widens the gap between automated and official timings. New times are assigned each time daylight appears between the riders, although the race rules ('*À chaque coupure effective, le chronométreur enregistre un nouveau temps*': At each *apparent gap*, the timekeeper shall record a new time) fall well short of the precision of the timing system, accurate to the thousandth of a second. A strung-out peloton can take half a minute to cross the line, and the official aggregate time of a rider who repeatedly finishes at the back of an unbroken group soon gains minutes on the sum of his uncorrected electronic readings. Further, if a rider crashes or experiences a mechanical problem in the final kilometre, he is given the time of the riders who were with him when it happened, provided he crosses the finish line eventually. If the final kilometre rule is extended to cover the final three or even five kilometres, as some contend it should be, the discrepancy between uncorrected and official timings could become cavernous.

The Prologue and time-trial stages are measured to the thousandth of a second, but only to compile accurate placings:

all electronic timings at the Tour de France are rounded down to the nearest second before being added to the general classification. In effect, these chronometric conventions question the credibility of individual timings in any sport. Events held in lanes on tracks and in pools are subject to slipstream effects and micro-environmental variations that create time differences unrelated to the athletes' performance; those in which athletes perform successively – downhill skiing comes to mind – are affected by changes in conditions over time. Far from introducing gratuitous approximation into reliable electronic timing data, the timekeepers restore the criterion of interdependence inherent in the slipstream, filing away at the raw electronic data like craftsmen finishing a masterpiece. When their job is done, the rider with the lowest accumulated time for the Prologue and all completed stages tops GC, and the rider who tops GC at the end of the final stage is the overall winner.

This austerity is in stark contrast with the multifarious striving after overall victory, points and mountains titles, young rider and team prizes, and the daily battle for the stage win – six simultaneous competitions fought out in four separate classifications. The over-abundance of enticements is completed by cash prizes at the intermediate sprints, mountain crossings and stage finishes and other *ad hoc* competitions including, for the Centenary Tour, the European Union Expansion Prize for the highest rider in the general classification from one of the nations to join the Union in 2004 (Estonia, Latvia, Lithuania, Poland, Hungary, the Czech Republic, Slovakia and Slovenia); and the Centennial Prize for the rider with the most consistently high stage placings at the 1903 Tour towns of Lyon, Marseille, Toulouse, Bordeaux, Nantes and Paris, necessitating yet another classification table. If, instead of anarchy, order – even elegance – emerges, perhaps it is because some deep-set generative logic is at play independently of this embarrassment of races.

Like Pharaonic death masks worn in an edifice built by anonymous workers, the category jerseys fix their wearers in Tour history. If the peloton suggests a primordial soup of souls, all longing to be made incarnate, to wear one of the brightly coloured category leader's jerseys, however briefly, is to be born into individuality. But in another of cycling's uncomfortable silences, the reasons why the jerseys are the colours they are are also lost to memory. Received wisdom is that the yellow jersey, coloured to match the newsprint of *L'Auto*, the newspaper that created the Tour, was first introduced on 19 July 1919. Awkwardly, in 1953, Philippe Thys, the winner of the 1913, 1914 and 1920 Tours, recalled wearing a yellow jersey in the 1913 Tour. Thys was sixty-seven at the time of his reminiscence and of sturdy memory. The points competition was created in 1953, the year of the Tour's fiftieth anniversary: the jersey may be green – although no one is certain – because its first sponsor was a garden supplier named La Belle Jardinière. The mountains competition has officially existed since 1934, although the chocolate manufacturer Menier had been offering cash prizes to the first riders up the great mountain passes since 1930. In 1975, a white shirt with large red spots was introduced to distinguish the mountains leader, representing, according to one uncon-firmed anecdote, colours worn by Lemoine and Guimbretière, two track riders managed in the 1930s by Félix Lévitan, co-director of the Tour de France from 1962 to 1986. The leader of the best young rider category wears a white jersey, which has drifted in and out of use, like the yellow caps once worn by the leaders in the team competition. Other individuals emerge from the rush of colour. The author of the previous day's most aggressive ride wears a red *dossard* or race number. Reigning world and national champions wear their champion's jersey; former national or world champions traditionally wear stripes in national colours, or the rainbow of the world championships, on the cuffs and collars of their team jerseys. The credible challengers for overall victory soon become recognisable, so too do the distinctively tall and short, the thickset and barrel-chested, the bearded, tattooed and the pierced. The injured are distinguished by their bandages. From the slowly differentiating mass of names and teams, the sub-competitions and the daily struggle for the stage win spawn more riders who may be granted temporary protection, or assigned one or more dedicated domestiques to accompany them. These riders too become recognisable because of the roles they perform and their position in the pack. Structure suddenly emerges everywhere.

The most visible competition of all, and the least trumpeted, is also the most decisive for the teams: the pursuit of airtime. The US Postal Service is one of twenty-seven businesses using the media exposure of the Tour as a gateway into the consciousness of global consumers. Unlike soccer or baseball clubs, which take the name of their host town, or Formula 1 teams, which are known by the car manufacturer, cycling teams are trade teams, known by the name of their principal sponsor, like racing yachts. As the peloton flashes past, it presents a dynamic image of economic activity in the main cycling nations. Five financial institutions, three brands of laminate flooring or carpets, three national lotteries, two telecommunications companies, two sportswear brands, a business consultancy and systems integration company, plus, from Italy, a wine producer and manufacturers of coffee machines, aluminium car wheels, goods for the construction industry and laminate metals; from France, a jewellery outlet and a croissant bakery; German mineral water, Belgian vitamin pills, a Basque supermarket chain and the regional administration of a major Spanish holiday destination – all flicker past like subliminal images inserted into a landscape sequence, infiltrating the bystander's memory. Only two have any intrinsic link with cycling: Euskadi, a foundation that supports cycling in the Basque Country, and the bicycle manufacturer Bianchi. The races within the race between teams sponsored by rival Belgian flooring companies or Italian grout producers are not immediately obvious, but are part of cycling's complex competitive mesh.

Naked commercial interest has always been part of the Tour. It, and the need for complex tables of data to understand the racing, underlie its very existence. For in the late nineteenth century, this meant either a blackboard or paper, and the earliest great cycling races, including the Paris–Rouen, first run in 1869, the Bordeaux–Paris and the Paris–Brest–Paris, both launched in 1891, were the creations of men of the press whose most pressing task was to sell newspapers: Richard Lesclide, the editor of *Vélocipède illustré*, Maurice Martin, his counterpart at *Véloce Sport*, and Pierre Giffard of *Le Petit Journal*. Cycling's commercial potential today is clear: even in the age of television, the weekend mountain stages attract two million or more roadside spectators. The spectacle is free. Publicity caravans give away boiled sweets, miniature cheeses and key rings that provoke a fervour and enthusiasm few forms of marketing can hope to emulate. In 2003 the gendarmerie compiled an official figure of 602,000 people watching the race on Alpe d'Huez alone, crowding the final fifteen kilometres on a stage of 211, all resonating with applause. The figure, of course, is a fiction, first, because great human masses evade enumeration as efficiently as termite nests, and second, because seeing the riders pass is one thing; discerning the race itself – that shifting field of vectors, now converging, now diverging, driven by a collective vitality – is another. Stadium sports use spatial boundaries to keep their network simultaneous: the contest reveals itself in real time within the spectator's cone of vision. Stretched out along a line cleaving to the topography, a cycle race is never fully present; it extends out of sight, revealing only fragments to the geographically fixed eye. These fragments make cycling perhaps the most accessible of sports, for no prior knowledge is required to be drawn to the stir of restless identities, or thrilled by their experiment with atmospheric friction, but form a lamentably pale impression of the burgeoning contest. The cycling fan requires more than attentive presence to follow the race's development. The spectators view a slice of action that they can place in context only later. In stadium sports, athlete and spectator cohabit simultaneous time; in cycling, only the athlete lives the race in the present: the spectator can see the action, but only follow the race retro-spectively. The crowds vacate the stadium knowing what they have witnessed. Descending from the mountainside, the cycling fan needs a high tolerance for uncertainty. The race is invisible; to witness and understand it, it must be reconstructed.

This reconstruction sometimes makes cycling seem quite inaccessible, although it is really no more complicated than some of the most popular sports in the global system. Stage races are decided by accumulated results over time, and their participants occupy relative positions in abstruse classifications; the same can be said of any league system. Given that it would be unprofessional for a domestique to divert energy from his team tasks into improving his position in the general classification, GC resembles a league in which the great majority of participants have no competitive interest. And unlike most sports, in which league or classification standings have a muted impact on individual games, cycling is hypersensitive to potential GC changes: who drafts, who works and who attacks can change from moment to moment according to what others are doing. In this, stage races are similar to the qualifying stages of tournaments like the FIFA World Cup, in which participants alter their tactics as results elsewhere change, even playing to lose in order to progress into an easier group. In most sports, this sort of behaviour is aberrant, a mismatch of mathematics and the sporting ethic. In cycling, it occurs daily. But a stage race is also like a marathon held over a much greater distance and duration, in which the onlooker needs to know not just who's ahead and who's behind, but who may have misjudged the pace. And, like tennis or chess, cycling results yield points for an under-lying world ranking system that decides, among other things, who receives an invitation to the *next* Tour de France – and who doesn't.

As well as the tables, akin to league standings in soccer, spectators need subjective assessments of the protagonists' physical state to make sense of the race's otherwise intangible structure. This information has traditionally been provided by newspapers: however, unlike journalistic accounts of stadium sports – essentially parasitic, reselling the event as nearly new nostalgia in the ensuing hours and days – newspaper descriptions of cycling races are part of the very structure of their apprehension by the public. For *Vélocipède illustré*,

Véloce Sport and *Le Petit Journal* and their successors, providing them has been a profitable business for a century and a half.

The Tour was born at the point where that precocious surge of sports publishing converged with a fierce and in some respects bizarre debate about the ethics of slipstreaming – bizarre, because the ethical aspect of gases wafting past aerofoils circumvent the standard university texts on fluid mechanics, and laboratory specialists would probably be surprised to hear their work has a moral component. Yet by demanding that riders choose between exploiting the front rider's work or cooperating with him, cycling transmutes the physics of slipstreaming into an ethical dilemma, one that generated a heated controversy in Paris at the start of the twentieth century when cycling, especially on the track, was extremely popular. The Vélodrome d'Hiver (constructed in 1892), the Buffalo at Neuilly (also 1892), the municipal track at Vincennes (1894) and then the Parc des Princes (1897) were four of nearly 300 velodromes built in France in the final decade of the nineteenth century to host races between bicycles, tricycles and tandems slipstreaming in every permutation as well as behind motorbikes, setting what some considered absurd records while, on the road, participants in the 580-kilometre race from Bordeaux to Paris, founded in 1891, drafted behind *entraîneurs* who went from bicycles to tandems, triplets and quadruplets – tandems for three and four riders – and finally, in 1898, to the motorcar. Madcap record attempts and outlandish machines pleased the crowds but detracted from the credibility of athletes. One of the parties to the slipstream controversy was the Baron de Dion, the wealthy patron of the bicycle and motorcar marque De Dion-Bouton: 'One day, leafing through a newspaper, I found a sports piece signed Henri Desgrange, answering an article of mine in which I argued that the velodrome slipstream events were no longer sport and should be suppressed. His admirably constructed response attacked me forcefully, but with great courtesy.' Desgrange was a former legal clerk who had set the first French hour record at 35.325 kilometres in May 1893, and created eight more records between then and 1895, including the hundred kilometre motor-paced tricycle, a perfectly reputable event at the time, at two hours, 41 minutes, 58.2 seconds – a record that still stands. The exchange between the two men might have come to nothing but for the Dreyfus affair. A Jewish army officer, Captain Alfred Dreyfus, had been convicted of spying for Germany on disputed handwriting evidence in December 1894. In 1897 new evidence, which appeared to exonerate Dreyfus, scandalised France and polarised public opinion. It drove apart old friends, including Pierre Giffard, owner-editor of the world's first sports daily, *Le Vélo*, and de Dion, who withdrew his advertising from *Le Vélo* and resolved to create a competing paper. Henri Desgrange's forceful style attracted him: 'It occurred to me that Desgrange could be one of the men I was looking for. I invited him for a talk and the result of our meeting was the creation of *L'Auto-Vélo* and his appointment as editor.'

Desgrange attracted a small team of devotees to the new journal, but their future was threatened when Giffard successfully sued *L'Auto-Vélo* for using the word *vélo*, his commercial property, in its title, and the Friday 16 January edition of Desgrange's paper appeared with its new, strangely truncated title, *L'Auto*. The following day, Desgrange announced a calendar of events for the year ahead, which included five automobile races, two athletics meetings, a swimming gala, rowing, fencing and weightlifting events, and four bicycle races, one of which was described as 'a great cycling road race of such interest that we will return to it in a series of special reports over the following days'. Géo Lefèvre, a staff reporter Desgrange had poached from Giffard, had actually come up with the idea of the Tour de France in November 1902, but no action had been taken. Now the journal staked its future on this unlikely scheme. So hasty was the planning that it was rescheduled twice in the following weeks. On Monday 19, the front page of *L'Auto* announced that the first Tour de France would take place between 1 June and 5 July 1903. A 24 February article brought stage one forward to 31 May. Then, on 6 May, the day after writing 'The number of entrants is still far from meeting our wishes,' Desgrange announced 'important modifications to the initial programme'. The event's duration was reduced from six to three weeks, the entry fee cut from twenty to ten francs, and the race put back to 1 July – a rescheduling that proved fortuitous thirty-three years later, when Léon Blum, France's first socialist premier, introduced paid July holidays and released a mass of spectators to enjoy the free spectacle. The final modification offered the first fifty riders in the final classification a reimbursement of ninety-five francs – five a day – to cover their expenses, provided, Desgrange added in a sadistic afterthought, they had averaged no less than twenty kilometres per hour on every stage.

The rules for the new event were formulated publicly in the pages of *L'Auto*. Desgrange had adopted de Dion's line on drafting; the vision that inspired him now was of solitary effort: victory should go to the strongest body; the thinking component should be minimised. Tactical acuity was a vice, not a virtue, at Desgrange's Tour. He referred to the riders as the *noblesse du muscle*: their minds didn't merit mention. He wanted to establish a simple, definitive pecking order among the riders. He couldn't have imagined that the drafting he so despised would allow the riders to interact with grace and beauty, nor that the pecking order he so desired could emerge with even greater clarity from the complex interactions made possible by teamwork. And, it is true, only a mathematician – and one conversant in some fairly cutting-edge forms of analysis, even today – could have predicted the emergence of formations into which the riders, whether attacking or chasing, and in spite of the contrasting aims that divide them, would spontaneously coalesce. The first of the configurations that characterise modern cycling is the 'Line,' a single file that speeds towards the top of the page like this:

$$
\begin{array}{cc}
 & L \\
\swarrow & R \\
R_1 & R \\
 & R \\
 & R \\
 & R \\
 & R \\
 & R \\
\end{array}
$$

One rider (L) assumes the load-bearing position at the front. When his energy begins to flag, he peels away (R_1), and rejoins the Line at the back. The Line maintains the speed a single rider can generate for the duration of his pull at the front. Its greatest asset is the long recovery time it allows. If there are nine riders, each works a ninth of the complete cycle and spends eight-ninths recovering – a highly economic formula that allows all nine to maintain a high speed for a long time at the smallest average energy expenditure to each. True, the load-bearer expends a great deal of energy; but provided all riders are committed to working, he also gets a long recovery period. The Line is the optimal strategy if all the riders in the group cooperate for the general good – if they are team-mates working ahead of their leader, or if they are in the early stages of a breakaway, working to establish a lead. The weakness inherent in the Line becomes apparent when the breakaway has become established, and the riders in it reappraise their commitment to the group. When this happens, the first shirkers appear among the workers, and in the Line, the shirker does extremely well. By taking a short pull at the front, or feigning fatigue and staying at the back of the group, in place of a gruelling work phase followed by a recovery phase eight times as long, the shirker enjoys up to seventeen recovery phases and stores energy while the workers expend it. This is why most Lines soon reorganise into an alternative pattern, not as good for the individuals in it, but immune to treachery from within. The Ball, or double file, in which one file of riders accelerates towards the front of the group as a parallel recovery file slips backwards, races towards the top of the page in the following shape:

$$
\begin{array}{cc}
 & \text{L} \\
\swarrow & \text{A} \\
\text{R} & \text{A} \\
\text{R} & \text{A} \\
\text{R} & \text{A} \\
\text{R} & \nearrow \\
\end{array}
$$

where the As are accelerating and the Rs are recovering. The moment each rider reaches the load-bearing position at the front of the acceleration file, he peels off into a parallel recovery file, loses ground until he reaches the back of the group, then rejoins the acceleration file and begins another journey towards the head. The Ball has the advantage of high speed, essential to opening a significant advantage, holding off a fast chase-down and allowing the air to settle in front of the chasing peloton. However, the high speed is matched by a high rate of energy depletion in the riders due to the low recovery time. Workers are better off in the Line, but shirkers do even better. Even in the Ball, the temptation to better one's own interests in a way that would be ruinous if everyone did so persists. Individuals will be allowed to miss a turn or two, for instance, if they have recently crossed solo from the chasing group. But the fast turnaround means defectors are quickly detected.

The Line and the Ball are both used by domestiques. After twenty-three kilometres of stage fifteen, the three CSC and four Cofidis riders who were leading the chase adopted the high-speed Ball formation:

	CSC
↙	CSC
CSC	Cofidis
Cofidis	Cofidis
Cofidis	↗
	Peña
	Padrnos
	Etc.

Ahead of them, the breakaway, which started with a Line, had also reverted to the Ball. From kilometre forty, Lance Armstrong rode in the hole behind Peña, Padrnos and Ekimov, who rode in the Line:

Peña

↙ Padrnos

Ekimov

↗

Armstrong

The need to establish a contract to share the load-bearing role at the front of the group generates these stable strategies of self-serving cooperation. The Line and the Ball are complex structures that can absorb shocks and reorganise. However, they never quite achieve equilibrium, and victory depends only on opening a momentary advantage at the right moment. Every stable state is, by consequence, temporary, and must sooner or later slip into chaotic flux. Psychological factors undermine the stability of the group from within: depleted energy levels in the riders, and the reputations and special-isations of the other riders in the group breed nerves. Envir-onmental factors push the stable state closer to its dispersion threshold: the approach of the chasing group from behind, the approach of the finish line or a geographical feature that disrupts the effectiveness of the slipstream – a long or steep climb or a fast and dangerous descent. When these factors combine, the breakaway enters a zone of instability in which the cooperation pact can fracture at any moment. A typical collapse occurs when a rider takes his few seconds of recovery at the back before tearing up the cooperation pact and surging away. The laws of physics suggest that it is a fool's move: the escape artist knows he will never outrun several riders in an organised chase; but he also knows that the moment a breakaway is established, its members' minds turn to planning their own individual coup. By contrast with the polite cooper-ation of the stable group strategy, the attacker abandons polite society with an act of piracy that condemns him to the company of outlaws. But only an outlaw will win: victory cannot stand too much cooperation. A lone attacker can rarely outrun an organised chase, but he may resist several riders if each is holding something in reserve for his own bid for victory. If two or more riders launch almost simultaneous attacks, a new cooperation pact between the members of this new, smaller group may emerge further up the road, and so on, until the stage is decided. The riders who miss the attack are left with a problem: there may be time to dart into its waning slipstream before it is swamped by still air, but whoever does so will drag his other breakaway companions along at greater energy expense to himself than to them. No one will want to be the first to counter-attack; the wise will wait and follow in the wake of the first to respond – which may mean that there is no counter-attack. If the attackers have timed it right, the chasers' individual ambitions will undermine their cooperation. There are any number of possible scenarios for what happens next; each depends on the collective sum of choices by the individual breakaway members. At any moment a choice presents itself: either to save energy and possibly lose, or to expend it and risk gifting another, more astute, rider the victory.

The evolution of cooperation in competitive cycling admits mathematical expression. What cannot even in principle be described mathematically is the breakdown of stability that produces victory, for two reasons: firstly, and practically, the variables involved, which include physiological data giving riders' energy and strength levels, cannot be measured during the race; secondly, and logically, any mathematical expression of the principles that generate victory would immediately become a value within itself – that is, the moment the equation was formulated it would immediately become one more strategic consideration in the strategy it seeks to describe. If the equation were extended to include its initial formulation, the new version would immediately suffer the same fate, and would have to be infinitely extended. It would recede for ever into undecidability. This potential infinity of outcomes gives cycling its sporting unpredictability. In stages one, two, four, five and twenty of the Centenary Tour, for example, the sprinter's teams timed the chase-down perfectly and mass sprints decided the stages. Stages seven, eight and nine were mountain stages, which always end with successful break-aways. The first flat stages to end in successful escapes were stages ten, which ended in a two-man sprint, and eleven, concluded by a fourteen-kilometre solo ride to victory.

No wonder, then, that the tactical delicacy of modern cycling was beyond Desgrange's powers of prediction. In any case, the conditions for the emergence of the domestique were not mature in 1903. Poor roads and loose-fitting clothing – the first Tour winner Maurice Garin rode in a white blazer – meant greater rolling resistance and skin drag. The freewheel, which allows drafting riders to recover by coasting with stationary pedals, had not yet been invented. All of this made drafting less efficient than it would become, and limited the domestique's utility. At the time, professional *entraîneurs* – literally, trainers or leaders – were still employed to provide a slipstream for suitable stretches of road. On 24 February 1903, Desgrange wrote:

The hottest issue to be resolved is the question of pacing. For years, constructors have objected to the alarming cost of maintaining pacers during road races. Riders too have protested that pacing as it is practiced today favours two or three and disadvantages the rest. There is no question of a man with no pacer or soigneur competing against those who are paced. We have therefore resolved to conduct the first five stages of the Tour de France without pacers, followers or soigneurs.

Desgrange clearly meant his race to create an alternative to slipstreaming. But he could not disguise his doubts, and added: 'The final stage from Nantes to Paris will determine the overall result: only this stage will allow pacers.' When the Tour finally arrived, article six of the race regulations stated: 'The race shall be held without pacers, soigneurs of any sort, or followers. However, the final stage from Nantes to Paris will be held with pacers. For the stage, only bicycle pacing will be authorised; any rider benefiting from any other type of pacing will be disqualified.'

The Tour was a resounding commercial success for Desgrange's newspaper. By timing the stages to meet its publishing deadlines, *L'Auto*'s circulation leapt from 25,000 before the 1903 Tour de France to 65,000 after it. On the day of the final, triumphant stage finish in Paris, 130,000 copies of a special edition of *L'Auto* went on sale seven minutes after the finish, and were sold within minutes. In 1908, Lucien Petit-Breton's second Tour win boosted *L'Auto*'s sales figures from 140,000 to a quarter of a million copies. During the 1924 Tour, it was selling 500,000 copies a day. The record circulation claimed by Desgrange was 854,000, achieved during the 1933 Tour de France. Inspired by *L'Auto*'s success, other newspapers followed. The international cycling calendar is full of events organised by, and named after, newspapers. The international cycling calendar has three three-week stage races: all three were the creations of newspaper editors: the Giro d'Italia originates from 1909 and Emilio Camillo Costamagna, editor of the *Gazzetta dello Sport*; and the Vuelta a España (1935) was the work of Juán Pujol of the daily

Informaciones. Seven of the ten one-day classics that collectively constitute today's World Cup were launched by newspapers. Dozens more newspaper-organised events take place all over the cycling world. The archives of these newspapers guard the memory of cycling, although even there the domestique is strangely absent. His story belongs to the historical category of figures and phenomena that leave no trace – the anonymous workforces who built Stonehenge and St Petersburg; the faces airbrushed out of photographs by censors in totalitarian regimes; the untellable history of perfect crimes. Yet human systems cannot fix the limits of history: chance or causality intervenes and the peripheral inevitably emerges. When the domestique steps into the light of memory, his heresy bears a family resemblance to that of the anonymous servant who lends his face to the mythological hero in some Renaissance masterpiece. In 1952, Sandrino Carrea, one of the domestiques who became known as 'Coppi's Angels', wore the yellow jersey for a day before his master Fausto took it from him and wore it into Paris, two weeks later. In 1963, Seamus Elliott became the first Irishman to wear the yellow jersey, riding on the team of the great Jacques Anquetil, who shortly afterwards took the jersey and the Tour. In 2003, the mystery face in the picture belonged to Victor Hugo Peña. His emergence began on the first day of the Tour, and in silence.

4

The Face in the Picture

Saturday 5 July 2003, 17:38: Eiffel Tower, Paris

From the starting ramp, I notice Johan is gesturing at me, mouthing something at me. Can you hear me? The radio isn't working. There'll be no way for us to communicate on the road. The Prologue to the Tour de France is an individual time trial, but individual time trials aren't as individual as they seem. It helps to have an outside observer who knows the route and can tell you when to conserve energy and when to expend it, when you should change gear, when to brake and when not to. Someone to pass on the split times of the riders who've gone before you so you know whether you're going fast or slow. Technical data, like a rally driver's co-pilot: 'Flat, five kilometres. Left-hand curve into 300-metre climb. Flat, two kilometres. Right-hand curve. Best time's . . .' The sort of thing you can use. You want to be in control. You don't want, 'That's it! Brilliant' or 'Come on, let's go. What's happening? What are you doing?' The crowd will tell you that. Information is what you need, and often, after a Prologue or a time trial, you think, They directed me well or, They directed me badly. Before radios, team cars were fitted with loudspeakers, which meant everyone could hear what you were being told. These days, no one uses a loudspeaker, and with no radio, I'll be information starved. I'm starting the Centenary Tour in silence, riding on instinct. Whatever I do now will show who I really am.

A month before the Tour, I was packing my things to fly back to Europe for a training camp when four men in black balaclavas burst in. They said they were guerrillas, and they'd been sent from the mountains. They said, 'The country is in conflict and either you contribute to the struggle or we take your brother.' They said they had information that there was $120,000 in my safe. I said, 'There is no safe. What you see here – the house, the car, the motorbike, the other car – is everything I've earned in my life. Take them if you want, but don't take my brother.' They started with a precise figure, but came down to $50,000, then less, and I realised they weren't guerrillas; they were common criminals. They took my suitcases and filled them with anything they could find. We were on the floor at gunpoint for three hours, and in those three hours I told them my life story. They were talking to me about poverty and suffering. I said, 'Ask after me in the village, and they'll tell you I was poorer than you.' As a child, I never went hungry, but we lived in one room, the four of us, until I was seven or eight. There was my parents' bed, my bed, and the cot where my brother slept. We put my father's bike down at night so that I could sleep, and during the day it lay on the bed when he wasn't using it. There was a kitchen for all the tenants, with three cookers, a small space for my mum's things. We borrowed a small space in the fridge to keep the milk and eggs. My father was a Telecom messenger. A postman, like me! Because he was a cyclist, he delivered the telegrams that were furthest away. One day each month, after my father had been paid, we bought the only luxury we allowed ourselves: a delicious, rich butter that we ate until it ran out, and then dreamed of until the following month. When I was eight or nine, I was ashamed that we lived in a single room paying rent, although it's common in Colombia. Eight or nine, and already worried about hiding the fact that we lived in one room.

Then my father was given funding by his company to enter the Tour of Colombia. He was always kind-hearted with cyclists, and told his boss, 'There's a rider who's younger and better than me. Let's send him with a masseur and a mechanic.' The rider's name was Helí Gutiérrez, eight or nine years younger than my father, who went as masseur, although they paid him all the same. Helí still has a paper cutting that says that he crossed the Alto de la Línea ahead of Lucho Herrera. He keeps it, although it's yellowed and fragile, so that people will believe him. My father never rode the Vuelta, but he was careful with the money, and saved enough to put a deposit on a house.

In 1980 there was a national junior cycling championship in Bucaramanga. I saw kids my age with little racing bikes, and I wanted one. My father eventually found one in a pawnshop. I still have it, a Raleigh with wide handlebars, barrel brakes and mudguards. I went with my father to the cycling meets, but from there you could see the swimming pool, and I decided I wanted to learn to swim. My father said, 'If you pass your exams, you can go to swimming classes.' After the first classes, they invited me to join the swimming club. My mother took me every day for eight years, normally at five in the morning. If she was tired or ill, she never let on. So I began this path in my life because of my parents. When I was fourteen or fifteen, I began to go on my own, and that's when I learned discipline: the discipline to train, and then come home. At parties with my schoolmates, I learned to say, 'I have to go and train.'

Meeting with my friends to do some schoolwork as a group, I did the group work, then: 'I'm sorry, I've got to go.' Then after school, a party, four boys, four girls: 'Sorry, I've got to go to train.' I did middle-distance events. I was national champion at the 200 metres breaststroke and the 200 and 400 metres medley from the ages of thirteen until I was seventeen. I held the departmental records until two or three years ago. They invited me to present the certificate to the kid who beat my records. In fact, for a cyclist, I breathe badly, because swimmers breathe through the mouth according to the rhythm of the stroke.

The 1980s were a golden age for Colombian cycling. I always felt close to cycling, because my dad was a cyclist. If we went to a hotel, everyone said, 'Hi, Hugo,' and I thought, 'Wow! They know my dad.' We went to the Tour of Colombia, and I stood on a curve and saw Manuel Cárdenas wink at my father as he rode past, and for me it was magical. And of all the kids at school or at the swimming pool, I was the only one who knew cyclists. If there was a race on TV, I was the only one who could understand what was going on – I knew that so-and-so was the leader in the mountains competition, and so-and-so had broken away and had a thirty-second lead. The other kids asked, 'Why is he doing this? Why are they doing that?' 'Wait. Lucho Herrera has broken away, and La Vie Claire is chasing him down.' 'Who's La Vie Claire?' 'The best team in the world.' I knew all those things. 'That's Greg Lemond. That's the jersey of Millar. And that's Eric Vanderaerden.' In 1995 I went on holiday with my father and our Renault 4 broke down right under the sign that says 'Alto de la Línea', the most famous climb in Colombian cycling. I wanted a photo of the sign, because for me it was like a myth. And my father told me, 'This is where so-and-so happened, and those curves down there are called El Cansaperros because they'll even wear out a dog – and here, such-and-such a thing took place.' I could already see myself there.

Being known as a swimmer made life difficult when I wanted to be a cyclist. People said I didn't have the physique, I couldn't climb. In the first physiological tests I had at the Postobón team in Colombia, the doctor said to me, 'You could win the Under-22 Tour of Colombia one day, but you'll have to build your legs, because you have a little girl's legs.' I had a swimmer's legs, not a cyclist's legs. When they measured me in Bucaramanga, I already had high oxygen absorption, an interesting cardiac rate, an athlete's physique. Swimming was excellent preparation. From eight to eighteen, I had the education of an athlete. Then I had to learn to suffer on a bike, to take the heat, cold, hunger, fatigue, the falls, and the hours and hours of effort twenty thousand times harder than swimming. Today it's hard to believe I swam four or five hours, ten thousand metres a day. Another life, another world. Stories about someone else.

My father's cyclist friends visited us by car, and I got the idea that cyclists joined a team and became millionaires. Then, one day, my mother broke the blender. We couldn't simply say, 'This one's broken. Let's go and buy another.' My mother was worried that day because she couldn't make fruit juice for us, but I said to her, 'Mum, when I'm a cyclist, I'll give you one as a present. When I'm a cyclist, I'll buy you anything you want.' And the day I received my first wage as a cyclist, I gave her a blender. It makes my hairs stand on end to remember. I have this great blessing from God. It doesn't matter to me if I don't earn a million dollars a month. I earn what I consider a lot of money, more than enough for what I want. Sometimes I phone my mother before I go home to Colombia, and I ask her what she would like me to bring. I'm prepared to buy her anything, and she'll say, 'Bring me some Spanish shampoo, and Spanish washing-up liquid.'

All this I said at gunpoint to the men who were robbing me. All this I have because of cycling. And some of it got through to them. I saw that they saw that I was right, although they were thinking, *We're here now, so we've got to go through with it*. That's what I could see in their eyes, because they could have done us harm, beaten us; they could have taken my brother, my parents or me. But I think they felt powerless, evil. They came to my house, and left feeling ashamed, as if they'd made a mistake.

Sport brings fame and wealth, but it can also distance you from your country, especially when you come from a developing nation. I've never wanted to live anywhere but my village, with the people who have always known me. When I meet old friends, I want to have normal conversations: 'How's your uncle, the guy with the smallholding in the hills? Do you remember when we went there, he had those cows ...' But they're already thinking, *How much did that watch cost? God knows how much he must earn*. When I was wearing the yellow jersey, and brought a moment of happiness to my country, I thought, *Everyone should do something for his country, small or large*. When my career is over, I'd like to do something for people in hardship. What do they say? – If you give a poor man fish, you feed him for a day, but if you teach him to fish, you feed him for the rest of his life. But when bandits break into your home and demand money, you wonder what sort of future you can have here.

They took documents, credit cards, my UCI health book. I had to change my papers, then found the Spanish Embassy had decided to issue no new entry visas to Colombians. I took them the deeds of the flat I own in Spain, the documents of my car, but they still said no. The Colombian ambassador in Spain called the Spanish authorities, and received the same answer. So I asked for a French visa, and they told me it would take at least a week. I had to call Johan and tell him I'd miss the Tour of Belgium. With a month to go to the Tour, my place in the team was in danger. I was given a French tourist visa, expiring 24 August. So I rode the Tour de France as a tourist, knowing that on 25 August, I'd be an illegal immigrant.

In the Prologue, one rider goes from each of the twenty-two teams, then the sequence starts all over again. The team directors decide who of their riders goes when. I said to Johan, 'Don't put me first. Put me at least in the middle.' And I'm in the middle. Our orders are to ride at top speed because the team time trial is just four days away. The starting order will depend on the team classification. The higher you are in the team classification, the later you start; and the later you start, the more split times you have to help you judge the pace. Provided stages one to three end in mass sprints and most of the peloton is given the same time, the team classification as it stands tonight will decide the starting order for the team time trial.

I saw the route for the first time at three o'clock, and rode around it three times. The first time I took a mental note of the curves, cobbles and potholes: the final curve, a fast ninety-degree right-hand bend over cobblestones, is technical – the cobblestones are more slippery than the asphalt. The second time, I tried to identify the best racing line. The third time, I clarified my ideas. Then I went to the bus and warmed up for an hour on the rollers. When you start to pedal, all sorts of things nag at you: your knee hurts, one of your shoes doesn't feel right, your skinsuit is tight. As you get into a rhythm, they dissolve: the suit begins to feel more comfortable, your knee stops aching, the saddle doesn't hurt any more. You're stretched out over the bicycle, coupled to it, thinking only of the cadence. You don't think about where your hands are or anything else, just the rhythm. You start off very gently then, after ten or fifteen minutes, you break into a sweat. You drink water to rehydrate and the body begins to wake up – the buffer chemicals that clear the lactic acid begin to circulate. You take the heart rate up then down again: when your pulse reaches 130, you accelerate, then at 170 you slow down. Some short, quick bursts loosen the legs, then you relax, turning them fast and strong. The body assimilates the effort. Then you do it again, three times. In the final ten minutes, you stick to the medium zone, 130 or 135, warm.

Lance hasn't been able to ride the Prologue route. He couldn't ride it with us at three o'clock because he starts at 19:07, and it was too early for his warm-up. He can't ride it now, because the race has started. So he's in the car with Johan. He arrived twenty minutes ago, and hardly anyone knows he's there. I'm aware it's Armstrong who's behind me. I want him to watch me, to sit there and watch me pedal, and perhaps say, 'This guy's pedalling well,' or 'He's going fast.' There are crowds shouting, screaming, applauding. There's a five-second countdown, then I accelerate down the ramp and away. I notice a Colombian flag near the start, but that's all I notice. The Prologue is so short, you don't think anything at all. You breathe in when you start, and you breathe out again when you cross the finish line. You're very quickly at the maximum your body will allow, and because the Prologue is short, you maintain it. Time trials are about maintaining a constant pace, like a continuous hum. But they are also about pain, an agonising heat you feel in the stomach, a burning that affects your breathing. You get into a rhythm, and when the pain comes, you tunnel into it, exploring it to the bitter end. Even the downward movement with my hand to reach my water bottle is going to upset the rhythm, so I often don't take on any water in a time trial. I remember the time trial I won at the Giro d'Italia in 2000. I felt that heat in the stomach, a pain like gastritis, and I said to myself, *Go with it to the end, to the very end*. That's what makes a time trial specialist – you feel that stinging in your legs, here, and you convert it into forward motion. You know it's linked to the fact that you're doing well. There have been times when I've wanted to ride a fast time trial, but I haven't been able to cross the threshold into pain.

My aerodynamic helmet comes down over my ears and amplifies the sound of the air rushing past. I don't hear the cars or motorbikes. If my earpiece was working, it would have to be painfully loud. What with the discomfort and the heat, some riders cross the finish line and throw their helmet down. I don't even think about it: it's all part of the same ache. From top to bottom, front to back, I gather it into a smooth ball of pain that spins around in my mind until the time trial is over – pain in my muscles, a burning in the sole of my feet, an aching in my wrists, a stabbing in my neck from holding my head in one position. There isn't a second to relax and stretch, or move my hands. I have to go on in the same position. If I want to spit, I do it by twisting my mouth sideways – tuh! – to avoid moving my head. I fix my eyes on an arbitrary landmark – a tree, a point on the curve – and I say, *Until I get there, I'm not going to change position*. And before I get there, I fix another point. After 3.2 kilometres, I see from the clock at the inter- mediate split that my time is close to that of the leader, Jörg

Jaksche. As I pass the split, I see the time: 3 minutes 48. The same as Jaksche. I must be going well. Seconds later, I see the sign that marks three kilometres to the end, and think to myself, *I can keep this going a few moments more*. Even during longer time trials, to resist moving my hand and reaching for water, I think about what I'm going to drink when I cross the finish line. It might be Coca-Cola or water, or natural lemonade. I begin to salivate because I know I'm going to drink something. The cobblestones at the end break my rhythm, but I also know we're all the same, we'll all get there at the same speed. It's important to be careful and not to fall. But at those moments you're not thinking anything. The final straight is a tunnel of sound: 7 minutes 30, 31, 32.240. Second on the leaderboard behind Haimar Zubeldia. The moment passes quickly: already I can't remember what I wanted to drink. I've forgotten the helmet was annoying me. Sometimes, when it's over and I've come second or third, and I think I could have gone faster on this curve or that climb or the descent where I was afraid, I wish I could go and do it again, even after the suffering and the strategies to cope. Two days ago – it must have been the day of the medical checks, at about five or six in the afternoon – I saw David Millar getting to know the Prologue route, with cars and everything, beside a police motorbike. By the first checkpoint, he was leading my time by seven seconds. If he hadn't lost his chain, he'd have won the Prologue by ten. In the end, he lost it by eight-hundredths of a second to Australia's Bradley McGee, a world champion on the track. I've never trained specifically for time trials. By preparing the Prologue, perhaps I could have ridden it faster.

Still, in the final three kilometres, I gained seven seconds on Jaksche. I'm happy with my time. It's a prize for me that Lance was behind me. Afterwards, he says, 'Man, you were fast. What gear were you using? What changes did you use? Is the curve there dangerous?' I tell him what I can, although I can't say what gear I was using because I couldn't look down to see. In a long time trial, there's time to look and see that the third cog in is a thirteen. But in the Prologue, it's hard to know. You know what gear you set off in, then you know you changed down one or two cogs. But after that you forget. Your legs tell you when to change down and when to change up. You go hard, or agile, but even if you're agile, you may be going so hard that you're pushing an eleven or twelve.

Later, when Lance passed the first split two seconds slower than me, someone said, 'You're going to beat Armstrong.' I didn't think so. I didn't think I'd beat Armstrong. As it turns out, I did, by a second – 1.31 seconds. Lance was in the car behind the team-mate who rode it best. Not just the team-mate: the fastest guy on the team. But it's only the Prologue, the first day, one of four in the same hotel. What matters is that for the team, it couldn't have gone any better. I was fifth, Lance seventh, Ekimov tenth. We are first in the team classification, and unless something unforeseen happens, we'll set off last in the team time trial, with the split times of all the other teams in our sights. After the Tour, when I begin to sum up my race, I'll be able to say, 'I rode a good Prologue, I did a Prologue ahead of Armstrong and the others.'

Prologue and General Classification
Total distance: 6.5 km
Leader's time: 7 mins 26 secs
Leader's average speed: 52.466 kph

					3.2 km	6.5 km	
1	MCGEE Bradley	FDJeux.com	96	AUS	3 mins 46	7:26.160	
2	MILLAR David	Cofidis	61	GBR	3 mins 41	7:26.240	same time
3	ZUBELDIA Haimar	Euskaltel-Euskadi	179	ESP	3 mins 47	7:28.252	2 secs
4	ULLRICH Jan	Team Bianchi	131	GER	3 mins 46	7:28.266	2 secs
5	PEÑA Victor Hugo	US Postal-Berry Floor	8	COL	3 mins 48	7:32.240	6 secs
6	HAMILTON Tyler	Team CSC	71	USA	3 mins 50	7:32.430	6 secs
7	ARMSTRONG Lance	US Postal-Berry Floor	1	USA	3 mins 50	7:33.550	7 secs
8	BELOKI Joseba	ONCE-Eroski	11	ESP	3 mins 49	7:35.330	9 secs
9	BOTERO Santiago	Team Telekom	21	COL	3 mins 52	7:35.400	9 secs
10	EKIMOV Viatcheslav	US Postal-Berry Floor	4	RUS	3 mins 49	7:37.020	10 secs

Prohibition!

Until 1927 and the invention of the team time trial, every stage saw great packs of riders darting from one slipstream to the next like silver fish in a shoal. Yet despite the difficulty of policing 360-kilometre stages with a couple of ungainly motorcars, Desgrange maintained his drafting ban for twenty-two years, even if doing so meant entertaining brazen contradictions. In 1909, despite the bar on teamwork, he accepted sponsorship from two publications, *La Vie au Grand Air* and *Annales Littéraires et Politiques*, to reward the team with the three highest-placed leading riders – the first team classification.

Without the means to enforce his ban consistently, Desgrange wielded it arbitrarily. In 1911, on the Pyrenean stage between Perpignan and Luchon, François Faber, whose six-litre lung capacity and improbable ninety-one-kilogram physique powered him to victory in the 1909 Tour, was nursing cholic, according to *L'Auto* correspondent Charles Ravaud, or an ankle injury, if we read Georges Rozet, Desgrange's personal guest. His Alcyon team-mate Maurice Brocco slowed until Faber could reach him, and began to pilot him forward to the lead group. In terms that no doubt echoed his host's indignation, Rozet wrote in outrage: 'The race commissaire, who spends the day watching out for this sort of friendly arrangement from his car, will take decisive action: Brocco will be disqualified tonight. By way of consolation, he has the right to ride one more stage while the French cycling federation, the supreme arbiter, ratifies Monsieur Desgrange's sentence.' On the following day's stage from Luchon to Bayonne, Brocco powered away and won the stage by thirty-four minutes, before leaving the Tour in disgrace.

A year later, Desgrange railed against the fine French rider Jean Alavoine in his report from stage five of the 1912 Tour de France. Eugène Christophe had 'put his nose on the handlebar at the stage start, not to lift it up for 360 kilometres', only dropping 'that parasite' Alavoine, 'whom he'd been sucking along in his wake', on the ascent of the Galibier. Alavoine was warned, but continued the Tour; in 1919, his compatriot Henri Pélissier walked out after similar treatment. After riding into a headwind for the first seventy-two kilometres of stage four, Pélissier, the race leader, stopped to tighten his headset. The Peugeot and Alcyon riders chose the moment to attack, openly taking turns at the front as in any modern breakaway. Pélissier began his 300-kilometre pursuit alone. By the time he reached L'Orient on the Atlantic coast, 145 kilometres into the stage, Pélissier was beginning to pick up the exhausted stragglers dropped by the leaders. Outside Nantes, he encountered Honoré Barthélemy, and the two men began to work together. Desgrange drove alongside to intervene. According to Tour historian Pierre Chany, who worked with Desgrange and Goddet and heard their oral accounts of the Tour de France, the conversation went: 'You're not permitted to slipstream.' 'Aren't the riders at the front slipstreaming?' 'If Barthélemy helps you, you'll both be penalised.' The following day, Pélissier abandoned in protest.

In 1910, Desgrange had vividly expressed the mindset that opposed him so trenchantly to slipstreaming and anything else that might mitigate the ordeal of professional road racing:

I should perhaps have ample reason to delight in the success of this eighth Tour de France, but rather than feeling joy, I'm troubled by a reflection: we have brought far too many riders back to Paris, and the numbers discarded *en route* are too small. This year, no serious cheating has been possible on the part of the slow and the uncompetitive who completed the race. However, forty-one of the 110 starters finished: it is, I repeat, far too many ... The Tour de France presents itself to the public as a gruelling trial: let us justify this opinion by placing new obstacles before our men. Less of them will reach Paris ...

The following year, he channelled the riders into the Alps and up the gruelling Galibier. The introduction of the freewheel predictably attracted Desgrange's scorn. In 1912 he raged:

Over the 379 kilometres of [stage eleven], the riders applied pressure on the pedals for scarcely half the distance. The rest was covered freewheeling. Behind the man who devotes himself to sustaining the pace, all our strapping fellows installed themselves as if on a sofa; they were sucked along, and covered enormous distances without any fatigue. The presence, I repeat, of men like Everaerts and Deloffre, Huret and Engel, for example, clearly indicates the ease with which they rode the stage. Is there any remedy? Are our races seriously threatened with decadence by the freewheel? Will the Tour de France be undermined by this infernal invention? Where will it lead? I well know that as far as *L'Auto* is concerned, the 1913 regulations will authorise the race director to suppress the freewheel in certain stages.

Yet, despite Desgrange's hostility, teamwork and drafting were already an integral part of the early Tours de France, as his own writing reveals. His report from stage nine of the 1913 Tour reads: 'Petit-Breton... has lost in the heat of battle six out of seven team-mates and can only count on Deman ...' – implying that the absence of a team would jeopardise his Tour.

However, in 1925, after twenty-two years like Canute, channelling his considerable resolve into holding back the tide, or, like Lear, into an unseeing rage, Desgrange was eventually compelled to accept what he called *esprit d'équipe*. He introduced two categories of racing licence:

Firstly, one allowing all riders indiscriminately to exchange or supply each other with [for example] food, small spare parts, light assistance in repairs; secondly, a licence applying only to the riders grouped into teams, permitted them to provide each other with very serious reciprocal aid (*une entr'aide très sérieuse*) which goes, for example, as far as waiting for a rider in the group who has just experienced a mishap and leading him by slipstreaming to the leading group ... Although the race is held without *entraîneurs*, followers and *soigneurs* on the road, each group of twelve riders constitutes a whole, within which the different members can provide reciprocal aid, in such a way as to arrive as numerous as possible, or to bring the marque they represent victory in the person of one or more of their members. Thus (the examples that follow are not exhaustive) a greater or lesser number of the riders on a single team, if one among them be distanced for whatever reason, may wait for him to lead him to the peloton.

The rules continue: 'This is the *esprit d'équipe* authorised by the rules. They do not prohibit an agreement within the group for a tactic (sprint, the train led alternatively by one or several members of the team) . . .'

The 1925 rule change allowed Lucien Buysse to emerge as the first great domestique in Tour de France history. Twelve years earlier, Buysse's brother Marcel had been leading the Tour de France when a broken handlebar had robbed him of his chances. Despite winning four of the six remaining stages, he could only claw his way back to third place overall. In 1925, after taking the race lead at Perpignan, the 1924 champion Ottavio Bottecchia delegated Lucien Buysse to take the lead and hugged his wheel all the way back to Paris. Buysse rode alongside him on the road to Toulon, opened the way for him through the hairpins of the Col de Braus, the Aravis and Galibier. For Bottecchia, the Tour ran smoothly, without crises or slip-ups. His shepherd Buysse even had enough left in the closing stages to take second place overall and give Automoto a one-two victory in the final classification. By 1926, Bottecchia was dead, apparently murdered by Blackshirts during a training ride, and Lucien Buysse was able to step up and win the longest Tour de France in history, a Tour in which no French rider won a stage. Desgrange complained that too many stages were decided by mass sprints, with the peloton arriving intact. After touching 500,000 during the 1924 Tour, *L'Auto*'s sales slumped for the first time since 1903. In 1927, Desgrange fine-tuned the rules yet again, creating twenty-four shorter stages and a striking innovation: team time trials in no fewer than eight of the sixteen flat stages, allowing individual riders the theoretical option of breaking away alone to obtain a better time. The team time trial was the product of Desgrange's sadism: he wanted to force every rider to ride flat out for the entire stage. It remains one of the great set pieces of the modern Tour de France.

The Rush of Nations

Wednesday 9 July 2003, 15:45: Joinville

The team time trial is a recipe for danger, locking small climbers and powerful *rouleurs* into a straitjacket formation at high speed with nothing more than a breath between us. If you have an itchy nose, you put up with it: the slightest random move can mean disaster. I don't think I drank at all during the stage: I didn't want to take the risk of reaching down for my *bidon*. In 2001, my first Tour, we had a fall. This year, we didn't want any mistakes. Ekimov was a track rider, George was a track rider, Pavel was a track rider, I was a track rider; we are strong in the time trial, and we grew up riding in tight formations. In 2002, we rode the entire stage in a Ball. It generates high speed – you race along at fifty-five kilometres per hour – but you work more rapidly; seconds after you finish one pull, it's time to start the next. You can't catch your breath; you can't recover. This year we used the Ball on the descents, because it allows you to ride at sixty-five where a single rider pulling at the front only goes at sixty, but formed a Line on the climbs and on the flat. Whoever started the climb, finished it. Whoever was leading into a village, pulled until we left it. You ride like cogs in a machine: the rider at the front maintains between fifty and fifty-four kilometres per hour, then, when he begins to tire, he peels away to the side and stops pedalling for two or three seconds. To help the riders further back in the line recover, the next to take over at the front doesn't accelerate; he simply maintains the same speed. The riders who have the most strength pull for two minutes. The riders who have less power may only pull for twenty seconds, but those twenty seconds will take them to the limit: we all go through the same hell. The team time trial is won and lost in the final ten kilometres, so it's crucial to keep the team whole. If only three riders have the strength to pull in the last ten kilometres, you aren't going to be as efficient as if there were six. If all you can manage is a few seconds, then you pull for a few seconds. There were moments in previous Tours when Lance was alone at the front on a climb doing the work of four or five and we were all recovering behind. This time, by mixing the two systems, we all did the same work, Eki, Pavel, George, Lance and me.

Hours after the Prologue had finished, my masseur Serge had brought up the subject of the yellow jersey: *If we win the team time trial, who'll be race leader?* It hadn't even occurred to me. My thoughts began to race. I began to play mind games with myself, rehearsing scenarios for the days to come. *I can't afford to lose any time tomorrow or the day after or the day after that, but if a breakaway gets clear, it can gain eight minutes, twenty minutes ...* I began to put myself under pressure. I tried not to get obsessed with it, but when I woke up the following day, and the next, and the next, it was all I could think about. Armstrong and Johan both said the same thing: 'I'd like to see you in yellow – but first, we have to win the team time trial.' And although I normally remember the stages – the climbs, the transitions between the climbs – the only memories of the team time trial that have stayed with me are the start, a few pieces of information we were told during the stage, Lance speaking to me, and the moment we crossed the line. The rest of the time I was concentrating so hard, I wasn't watching to see if it was straight, or a climb.

There were three splits. At the first, after eighteen kilometres, we could see the clock: we were sixth, fourteen seconds behind the leaders, Team Telekom, and six seconds behind ONCE. Lance said to me, 'I need more.' Twenty-six and a half kilometres later, ONCE had taken the lead, and we were in second place, six seconds back. I was convinced we were going to lose, and I thought to myself, *This can't be happening*. At the third split, there was no clock, so one of our *directeurs sportifs*, Dirk Demol, asked a friend to wait with a stopwatch. I heard Dirk say, 'He'll be there ten kilometres from the finish to give us the split time.' I didn't know Dirk's friend, but when we passed the split point, I saw an old man with white hair and a stopwatch in his hand, giving us the thumbs-up. It had to be him. We had a seventeen-second lead over ONCE, which meant we had gained twenty-three seconds on them in the fifteen kilometres between the second and third split. I couldn't help thinking, *We could still fall, I could still puncture*, and my nerves got bad. I don't remember anything of the final ten kilometres. But I think there were two riders in me pedalling: one who wanted to win the stage for the team, and one who wanted to win the yellow jersey.

Léopold Alibert, Peugeot's *directeur sportif*, guided his riders to victory in four successive Tours between 1905 and 1908. Alphonse Baugé directed the great Alcyon teams to success each year from 1909 to 1912, then steered Peugeot to victory in 1913 and 1914, and La Sportive, the Peugeot and Alcyon merger, in 1920. Ludovic Feuillet directed the winners for Alcyon between 1927 and 1929, before steering Belgium to victory in 1935. Objecting to any tactical component other than riding all out, Desgrange took the success of the great pre-war *directeurs sportifs* as a personal affront. In 1929, a solidly built twenty-eight-year-old from Flanders named Maurits Dewaele took a comfortable fifteen-minute lead before the race left the Pyrenees. In Grenoble he was so ill that he could only take in sugar dissolved in water, yet with the help of his Alcyon team-mates, he preserved his lead to Paris. The sight of a sick man winning the Tour de France thanks to the all-powerful cycle manufacturers was too much for Desgrange. To make matters worse, sales of his newspaper were in decline. Something had to be done. In 1930, he introduced national teams using equipment provided by the organisers. Intensified national radio coverage increased the value of advertising for the paying members of the greatly enlarged publicity caravan, which paid for the new-formula Tour. Desgrange meant to harness national passions for the benefit of the Tour: the Tour, however, sometimes struggled to contain them. In 1937, after two straight Belgian Tour wins, roadside hostility during the stage from La Rochelle to Bordeaux led the Belgians to withdraw. The following year, Mussolini exploited Gino Bartali's outstanding victory as a propaganda coup for Fascism. And as war brewed in 1939, Italy and Germany boycotted the Tour. After the Second World War, in 1949, French riders claimed they had been insulted and stoned by Italian fans when the race entered the Val d'Aosta. The following year, the Italian team withdrew after Gino Bartali was manhandled by French crowds on the Col d'Aspin. Yet, despite these excesses, Desgrange's reform was a massive success; from 1930 to 1934, the French national team achieved five successive victories, largely thanks to teamwork, and won the Tour unprecedented popularity and national interest. Jean Antoine's radio reports, extensive newspaper coverage (during the 1933 Tour, *L'Auto*'s circulation reached that record of 854,000) and, from 1936, paid workers' holidays, cemented the place of the Tour in the French national consciousness and the international sporting calendar.

The national team format accelerated the internationalisation of the Tour, a process which would ultimately make even national teams obsolete and replace them with truly global formations like the US Postal team. This tendency is as old as the race itself, despite its origins as a half-cocked publicity stunt for an ailing national newspaper. The Olympic Games and the FIFA World Cup, to name two comparable French inventions, had been conceived as congresses of nations; the Tour had internationalisation thrust upon it. Until 1947, it stayed within France's borders, with the exception of irregular visits to German-occupied Metz and French-speaking Geneva. Even today, when it attracts a global TV audience in over 170 countries and riders from around the world, most of the race takes place in France, the great majority of roadside fans are French, and the organisers are the French successors of Desgrange and Lefèvre. The first of these was Jacques Goddet, whose father Victor had been the financial comptroller of the Parisian velodromes at the first Parc des Princes and the Vélodrome d'Hiver, and after 1900, of *L'Auto*. Jacques Goddet created *L'Équipe* on *L'Auto*'s demise after the Second World War, in association with Émilien Amaury, the owner of the newspaper *Parisien Libéré*. Amaury sent an agent to assist Goddet, but also to keep him in check; his name was Félix Lévitan. Goddet and Lévitan were an odd couple. Lévitan had risen from lowly social status through hard work and a driving ambition. Goddet regarded him as a parvenu. Goddet delegated responsibilities; Lévitan issued curt orders: '*Il faut se soumettre ou se démettre,*' was his central precept – 'Follow your orders or find another job.' Lévitan was a devoted husband all his life; Goddet had four wives and observed: 'I always wanted to marry the woman I loved at the moment I loved her.' Lévitan was prompt; Goddet was frequently late. The rows between them were legendary. Their uneasy collaboration ended only in 1986. For two years, a former civil servant named Xavier Louy assumed the race direction after eleven years spent managing its internationalisation. Louy's distinction is to have designed the 1989 route, which yielded the closest finish in Tour history when Greg Lemond beat Laurent Fignon by eight seconds. Then, a distinguished sports journalist (and former professional cyclist) named Jean-Marie Leblanc was appointed in 1989. Leblanc remains at the helm at the start of the twenty-first century.

Cycling races are often credited with teaching national populations their country's geography. Historians have suggested that the hand-drawn route map of the first Tour de France published on the front page of the 26 June 1903 edition of *L'Auto*, risibly scruffy and homespun by today's technological standards, was among the institutions that gave the French an engrained image of their country's outline, and an accessible photographic record of its landscapes. But the Tour de France offers more: an education in the nations of the world. At the first Tour in 1903, just five took part – France, Italy, Belgium, Luxembourg and Switzerland. The Tour de France soon became a rush of nations, and by the First World War, eleven had competed: France, Belgium, Switzerland,

Italy, Germany, Luxembourg, Algeria, Spain, Tunisia, Denmark and Australia. The influence of the Berlin Olympics led to a false expansion: in 1936, a record ten nations competed, and Yugoslavia, Romania and the Netherlands became the sixteenth, seventeenth and eighteenth nations to participate. The Yugoslavs and Romanians quickly abandoned; the next Yugoslav rode in 1986, the Romanians never returned. By 1939, the Tour had drawn on nineteen nations, just three of which – Romania, Monte Carlo and Tunisia – were not retained. The remaining sixteen – France, Belgium, Switzerland, Italy, Germany, Luxembourg, Algeria, Spain, Denmark, Australia, New Zealand, Japan, Austria, Yugoslavia, the Netherlands and Great Britain – all came back. Since 1947, thirty new nations have been represented. Of these, two – Morocco and Liechtenstein – made only fleeting appearances in mid-twentieth-century Tours and never returned, and three – the Saarland, Czechoslovakia and the USSR – ceased to exist. The rest came in waves. The first, between 1947 and 1960, we could call the 'Wave from the European Extremities', bringing riders from Poland, Ireland, Portugal and Sweden. Between 1975 and 1991, a second – the 'New World Wave' – flooded in, bringing the first representatives from Colombia, USA, Canada, Brazil and Mexico, as well as the first Norwegian. The 1979 record of sixteen nationalities was broken seven years later when twenty nationalities were represented at the 1986 Tour, thanks largely to this invasion from the Americas. In 1990, the Tour de France invited a team of Soviets sponsored by Alpha-Lum – although the sponsorship money bypassed the riders, whose rouble wages reduced them to penury. Since then, a 'Great Eastern Wave' has brought representatives from Russia, Ukraine, Slovenia, Latvia, Moldova, Uzbekistan, Lithuania, Estonia, Kazakhstan, Slovakia, Hungary and Croatia, as well as Venezuela, Finland and South Africa, to international cycling's now global community of nations.

At the first Tour in 1903, six French riders took part for every foreigner. By 1919, the ratio of French to non-French riders was one to one. In 1925, foreign nationals outnumbered French riders for the first time. In 1934, there were two foreign nationals per French rider. In 1963, French riders were outnumbered by an individual nationality – Belgian – for the first time, and the ratio of foreign-national to French riders reached three to one for the first time. At the 2003 Tour, foreign riders outnumbered French riders by about four to one.

Success, too – in terms of stage wins, category wins, taking the race lead and (since 1919) the yellow jersey, finishing among the top three overall, or winning the Tour outright – has been internationalised. Of the fifty nationalities that participated in the Tour between 1903 and 2003, thirty-three have won at least one stage, twenty have worn the yellow jersey, nineteen have finished on the final podium, ten have won the points competition and ten the best young rider title, nine the mountains prize, eight the best team title, and eleven the Tour itself. The internationalisation of Tour de France success is another history of waves of nations sweeping in, achieving their first successes and building on them, before another wave crashes in. Representatives of France, Belgium, Italy and Luxembourg won every Tour until the 1940s. Switzerland joined this exclusive club in 1950; Spain, only in 1959.

However, the true globalisation of success at the Tour de France began only in 1981, marked by the moment Australia's Phil Anderson became the first non-West European to wear the yellow jersey. Between then and 1987, five other nations from outside Western Europe enjoyed their first successes:

Colombia, the USA, Canada, Mexico and Poland. Norway was also swept in by the same wave. In 1990 and 1991, riders representing the Soviet Union, Brazil, then former Soviet athletes now riding for Russia and Uzbekistan joined the party. In 1994 and 1995, riders from Latvia, Slovakia and Ukraine began to make an impact on the Tour. In 1998 and 1999, the Czech Republic and Estonia and in 2002 and 2003, Lithuania and Kazakhstan entered the roll-call of successful Tour nations.

As the Tour internationalised, so did the surrounding sporting environment. Henri Desgrange had been aware of the international context: the success of the Bologna–Ferrara individual time trial in the 1933 Giro d'Italia predated the first individual time trial at the Tour in 1934. In 1948, the Tour was included in an international competition created to determine the world's number one rider. The Challenge Desgrange-Colombo was organised by the newspapers *L'Équipe*, *La Gazzetta dello Sport*, *Het Nieuwsblad-Sportwereld* and *Les Sports*, bringing together the principal one-day classics, plus the Tour de France and the Giro d'Italia. Compiled between 1948 and 1958, the Challenge Desgrange-Colombo was the forerunner of both today's World Cup and the UCI world rankings system. Disagreements between French and Italian organisers brought the demise of the Challenge Desgrange-Colombo. It was replaced by the Super Prestige Pernod International, which became a true international competition in 1961, based on results in both classics and stage races, and lasted until the French ban on sports sponsorship by alcohol brands in 1988.

The Tour entered another network of international connections in 1949 when Fausto Coppi completed the first Giro d'Italia–Tour de France double. The Giro–Tour double has been part of the ambition of every three-week tour champion to date except the Americans Greg Lemond and Lance Armstrong. It was achieved by Jacques Anquetil in 1964, Eddy Merckx in 1970, 1972 and 1974, Bernard Hinault in 1982 and 1985, Stephen Roche in 1987, Miguel Induráin in 1992 and 1993, and Marco Pantani in 1998.

But the Tour's greatest internationalist was Jacques Goddet. In 1958 he told the magazine *Miroir-Sprint*: 'My intention is to internationalise the Tour de France as far as possible. I'll only succeed by maintaining, at all costs, the principle of national teams – the only formula capable of enlarging the field of relations with foreign nations, and especially those of the East, whose representatives I hope soon to see participating in our race.' But by 1961, Goddet had to recognise that national teams were becoming an anachronism at the Tour, as trade teams were disputing every other major cycling race. So he transferred the formula to an amateur stage race, the Tour de l'Avenir, integrated into the spectacle of the Tour, which it preceded by two hours. The Tour de l'Avenir consisted of fifteen days of competition over reduced distances with respect to the stages of the Tour de France. It was disputed between national teams and conducted according to Goddet's stipulations for fifteen years, and became a training course for amateur riders aspiring one day to ride the Tour de France. Trade teams disputed the Tour de France for five years between 1962 and 1966, but in 1967 and 1968 Goddet returned to his cherished national teams, before admitting defeat the day after the end of the 1968 Tour: 'As things stand, only five nations can send competitive teams. Teams sponsored by marques, it seems to me, are the most natural and homogeneous entities.' Still, Goddet's internationalising policies were so successful that today, national teams would limit, not increase, the number of nationalities taking part in the Tour de France.

Nonetheless, even under Goddet's leadership, the Tour was not indisputably the greatest cycle race. In May 1957, the Frenchman Louison Bobet, wearing the leader's jersey of Italy's national tour, announced that he would not take part in the Tour de France. Bobet's iron discipline, unforgiving work ethic, three Tour de France wins and the World Championship he had won in 1954 on German territory had made him a living symbol of France's post-war recovery. It was unthinkable that he should prefer the Giro to the Tour. Merckx repeated the slight in 1973, deciding not to defend his title at the Tour after completing a historic double by winning the Tours of Spain and Italy in the spring.

Only the globalisation that began in the 1980s has allowed the Tour to establish its primacy at the heart of the cycling calendar. By 1984, the French cycling magazine *Vélo* created a points table inspired by the APT system used in tennis. It identified a World Number One cyclist and allowed every professional in the world to be classified. The system was adopted in modified form by the UCI. Cycling was now an integrated global system, but a curiously unbalanced one. At the hub of the system is the Tour de France, incomparably more important that either the World Championships, or the World Cup, created in 1989.

Cycling, then, has become a global sport thanks to its organisers. It took a rider to elevate the sport into the common currency of global popular culture: that rider is Lance Armstrong. Sure, Orson Welles waved off the 1950 Tour de France and Dustin Hoffman accompanied the 1984 race in preparation for a film, *Yellow Jersey*, that was never completed; but Armstrong has connected the riders themselves to an international culture only the huge US market has the economic power to sustain. He has attracted advertising deals from pharmaceutical companies, hotel chains and car manufacturers (sectors little tapped by cycling), he has brought movie stars such as Arnold Schwarzenegger and Robin Williams to the Tour, and even been romantically linked with famous actresses and music stars. Truly an American success story, although, as Armstrong himself says, 'If I'd just won the Tour de France and didn't have cancer, the story wouldn't have been told as much. It was major for cycling but also for cancer: the combination of the two made the story.'

This Americanisation of the Tour de France is reflected in the race results. The rate of the internationalisation of success at the Tour during the final quarter of a century is almost four times faster than the rate during the Tour's first twenty-five years. During the first twenty-two Tours, just five nations – France, Switzerland, Belgium, Luxembourg and Italy – shared all the indicators of success. Luxembourg, in particular, achieved enormous success, despite the tiny number of riders who took part: three years after François Faber became Luxembourg's first representative at the Tour, he won its first Tour de France. By 1928, Luxembourgers had attained three Tour wins after just twenty-one starts by eight individual riders – a success rate of one Tour win for every seven starts. The Luxembourg of the final twenty-five years of the Tour's first century is the USA. The first US participant was Jonathan Boyer in 1981 (he was also the first to use a bike computer at the Tour). Three years later, an American finished on the podium (and everyone had a computer!). Within five years, Lemond had won the Tour. Of just 115 participations by US riders, eight have produced a win – a success rate of one Tour win for every 14.375 starts. Compare these with France's thirty-six wins in 4690 starts, a success rate of about one win for every 130 participations. By this standard, it is time Great Britain (136 participations between 1937 and 2003: no wins) won the Tour. A Colombian win (180 participations 1983–2003: no wins) is long overdue.

The nineties was the only decade in Tour history to see regular and consistent growth in the number of nationalities represented at the Tour: twenty-one in 1992, twenty-three in 1993, twenty-four in 1994, and twenty-six in 1996. 2002 saw a record thirty nations represented, proving Goddet's conversion to 'teams sponsored by marques' well-founded. The interest created by this now global event is reflected in the number of nations that receive TV coverage: since 4 July 1961, when Italian TV broadcast the stage from Grenoble to Turin, international television coverage of the Tour de France has expanded at a dizzying rate. By 1992, the Tour was being broadcast in seventy-two countries. A year later, 119 countries saw it. This figure was 152 in 1994; by 1997 it had increased to 160.

A hundred and seventy-two nations are receiving television images of the Centenary Tour, and among the twenty-six nationalities taking part, three are taking small steps forward in their sporting history. Vladimir Miholjevic of Alessio is the first Croatian national to ride the Tour; while Kazakhstan, already firmly established in professional cycling, will take its first stage win in the coming days, thanks to the muscular Alexander Vinokourov, challenging for his nation's first finish on the podium in Paris. As yet, no Colombian, or any rider from any developing nation outside the Eastern Bloc, has worn the yellow jersey. But the US Postal team, with Victor Hugo Peña taking long turns at the front, is still racing towards the finish line.

Into History and Out Again

Wednesday 9 July 2003, 16:52: Saint-Dizier

The final ten kilometres were our strongest. As we approached the line, I tried not to smile, to laugh. We had almost doubled our lead over ONCE, and finished thirty seconds ahead of them. Ullrich's Team Bianchi was third, forty-three seconds behind. The team time trial is my discipline: I was one of the strongest riders who contributed most to winning the stage. I shouted in triumph as I finished. I was the new leader of the Tour de France.

Lance embraced me. Everyone congratulated me, shook my hand. But the yellow jersey brought me into conflict with our press officer, an ex-rider named Jogi Müller. I saw the Colombian radio commentators Alfredo Castro and Hector Urrego. Alfredo was half shouting, half mouthing at me across the compound: 'The telephone ... Come to the telephone.' I went over to talk to my country live. It was then that Yogi interrupted and took the phone out of my hand: 'They're not accredited.' I tried to shrug him off, but he was adamant. 'The journalists at the official press conference have paid to be there, and you have things to do.' To me, they were the most important journalists at the Tour. They've been following us

The Prologue: 'You breathe in when you start, you breathe out again when you cross the line. In between, you fix your eyes on an arbitrary landmark and you say, "Until I get there, I'm not going to change position." And before you get there, you fix another point.'

The Team Time Trial: 'A straitjacket formation at high speed with nothing more than a breath between us. The riders who have the most strength pull for two minutes. The riders with less power may only pull for twenty seconds, but those twenty seconds will take them to the limit: we all go through the same hell.'

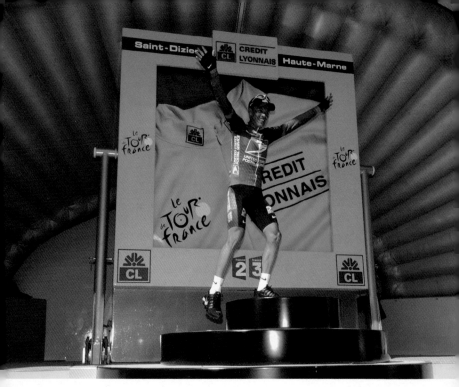

Above, Victor Hugo Peña on the podium of the Tour de France, about to receive the yellow jersey the day before his twenty-ninth birthday. *Left*, before a smaller, less global audience, aged ten. To his left, his childhood friend Daniel Duarte: 'When we were kids, we'd pretend we were our favourite cyclists: the game could be football, or anything, but he'd be Lucho Herrera and I'd be Fabio Parra.'

Two Teutonic giants at the 2003 Tour de France. *Right*, at Toulouse: Arnold Schwarzenegger meets the US Postal team. *Below*, on the climb to Ax-3 Domaines: Jan Ullrich (*right*) increases the pressure on Lance Armstrong, beside the swashbuckling Kazakh, Alexander Vinokourov (*left*).

Above, Hugo Peña Moreno, Victor Hugo's father, a Category 'A' rider in the Bogotá League in 1973, waits for a wheel on the Alto de la Tribuna north of the Colombian capital. *Below*, stage 15: Victor Hugo on the Tourmalet: 'Mikel Artetxe is ahead of me. I whisper to him, "Take it easy, Mikel, recuperate, catch your breath, Mikel, relax, so that I can catch mine."'

'Why is it that everything happens to Lance?' *Above*, stage 15: the fall on the climb to Luz Ardiden. Victor Hugo sees the replay on the TV in an ONCE team car during the stage. *Right*, the end of stage 19, the Pornic-Nantes individual time trial in the pouring rain. Lance Armstrong knows at last that he has won the Centenary Tour de France.

The idea of a Tour de France was elaborated here in November 1902. A century on, the walls are lined with artificial US sports memorabilia. Considerable efforts have clearly been made to wipe away all traces of history and replace them with a fantasy past that pales beside the truth. An old pig-iron bike – as far from a racing bike, even an early racing bike, as could be imagined – hangs from the ceiling, in front of a photograph of Maurice Garin, cut from a magazine.

to Europe for decades. My yellow jersey also belonged to them, yet they were at the bottom of the official heap. Later, the President of Colombia called. I wasn't allowed to take the call until I had our press officer's permission. He told me, 'Thank you for giving Colombia five minutes of peace.' Afterwards, the press officer came to my room and found me talking to a journalist from Colombia. He took the telephone, and said into the mouthpiece, 'Two minutes.' I thought to myself, *I'll talk to whoever I want*. But afterwards, he sat down with me and explained himself: 'A journalist comes to me and says, "I want to speak to Victor Hugo." I say: "He's having dinner now, but you can speak to him from eight to ten past." Then someone phones and you spend half an hour speaking to him. It takes my authority away.' It took me a while to understand that he had a job to do, and I apologised.

On the bus, I waited until everyone had gone, because Lance is always the last off. He might have been thinking, *What happens if he tries to keep the jersey?* I wanted him to know my thinking wasn't going to get twisted. I wanted to say, 'This yellow rag's yours. Thank you for giving me this opportunity. Thanks for lending it to me for a while: you don't know what it means for my country. For a moment I feel some of the things you feel,' is what I wanted to say. The press wanted to hear something controversial: of course I'd have liked to keep it a few more days, but I wasn't going to win the yellow jersey; I had come to help the best cyclist on earth win the Tour. He just said, 'It's yours. You earned it. I gave you nothing.'

In the dining room that evening, I was almost ashamed: to my team-mates I was still just me. Over dinner, they joked, 'Victor Hugo, what have you done?' 'Who'll be able to put up with you now?' 'You're the King of Colombia.' But it wasn't malicious: they were genuinely happy for me. It was difficult to sleep that night, not because of the pressure, but because of the happiness. I wanted to sleep, but I started to think about how many riders had come before me, perhaps better riders than me, and never wore the yellow jersey – not even as a present. They never had the opportunity to ride for a team like this. I lay there thinking all these things, instead of sleeping.

We cyclists live our lives like monks or prison inmates, saturated by the discipline the sport imposes. During races, the day and date mean nothing to us. Only the stage number counts, and when the rest days are. For me, there's one exception: 11 July, my birthday, and this year it was the day after the team time trial. I was congratulated by Ullrich, Garzelli, Millar, McGee. Every so often I felt a pat on the shoulder and, 'Congratulations!' Even at high speed, in difficult moments, I continued to hear, 'Congratulations!' I said 'Thanks' with whatever breath I had left. From that day on, I heard another name at the roadside. Not just Armstrong or Richard or Ullrich, but fans shouting, 'Allez Peña, allez Victor Hugo,' 'Pena', or 'Piña', or 'Victor Hugo'. And afterwards they recognised me: 'Look, he was the yellow jersey – Peña, isn't it?' And I thought, *I have a place at the Tour now*, because the previous two years, although I'd participated in the Tour, although I'd finished tenth in the final time trial in 2002, and second in the team time trial, and been part of the US Postal team, I'd left no mark. This year, when I was leader, I heard my name and I felt in those moments that I existed for the Tour. At one point that day, I said to Lance, 'Can we stop for a piss?' and he said, 'We do whatever the yellow jersey wants.' I didn't feel I had the authority – maybe they'd attack when I stopped. But Lance said, 'Whatever the yellow jersey wants,' so I stopped. And everyone stopped. It was fantastic! For three days, I had all the authority of the yellow jersey. I remember an old Frenchman at the start one day, who said – and although I don't normally understand French, I understood very clearly – 'What you've done is very special. Not even Raymond Poulidor wore that yellow jersey. And look how great Raymond Poulidor was.' And I thought to myself, *Poulidor, and who knows how many of the greats, never wore the yellow jersey. And how many great riders to come will never wear it?*

On the stage to Lyon, it was very hot, and with twenty or twenty-five kilometres to go, I was thirsty. I was going to ask a friend on another team for water when I saw Armstrong had no water bottles. And I thought, *I can't ask a friend to give me water for the race leader – lukewarm water ... Lance never issues orders to anyone.* But although the race was very fast, I thought, *I can make it*, and I set off for the back of the peloton. You need to know how to dose your energies for those rides back for water. You try to go when everybody needs it, so that it's worth the effort. Ekimov, Pavel, Floyd and I had to be at the front, so it was up to George, Rubiera, or Triki to bring us water. Sometimes, you'd say, 'I'm going for water,' and one of the other riders would say, 'I'll go.' I took six or seven bottles and crammed them into my yellow jersey, then said, 'Right, let's see if I make it back to the front.' It was another time trial past nearly 200 cyclists, each 1.5 metres long, stretched out in a long, fast line, chasing a breakaway that was still two minutes ahead of us. As I passed Iván Parra, I asked him, 'What do you think? Have I lost it or will I keep it?' He said, 'You'll still have it ...' Rubiera said the same thing. I made it and handed out water to the guys up front, all but two riders, I think. I gave the water to Lance, who looked at me in astonishment and said, 'Thanks.' I think they were the most sincere thanks I've ever received in my life.

With ten kilometres to go to Lyon, I wasn't so sure I'd keep the jersey. The team wasn't going to waste energy defending it knowing that the mountain stages were about to start. Fassa Bortolo was pulling at the front, going really fast, and in the last seven or eight kilometres you could practically see the breakaway riders thirty seconds ahead of us. We came to a small climb, and some of the Fassa Bortolo riders began to fall back, leaving others isolated at the front. I tried to remain calm, but there was a moment in which I was so desperate I said, 'No, this can't be. I can't lose the jersey. One more day ...' and I reached out and pushed one of them, so he wouldn't drop any further back. Then another started to drop back on the other side, and I pushed him too – I put my hand out to push him so that he'd make it over the climb and carry on working at the front. I don't think they knew who'd pushed them; they probably thought that it was one of their team-mates giving them a little hand over the climb, but I reasoned that if I didn't help them, they'd be a long way back by the end of the climb, and by the time they got back to the front I could have lost the jersey. So they carried on pulling, and in the last two or three kilometres, they caught the breakaway.

Then, we reached the mountains. The first mountain stage set off from Lyon, over some category two and three climbs, then up the Col de la Ramaz, a first category monster, before a long descent to Morzine. My job was to work at the front from Lyon to halfway up the Ramaz. I was strong that day, strong enough to have kept the yellow jersey another day. I could have joined a breakaway, or said, 'I can't work, my leg hurts.' But my job was to ride the first five kilometres of the Ramaz for Lance, and I made sure I was the first to get to work, because that was my job. I wasn't thinking, *I'm the yellow jersey. I'll climb close to Lance, lose as little time as possible and keep the yellow jersey*, or, *I'll try to stay in the top ten, or the top twenty*. In cycling, if you're not the winner, you're a loser; no one remembers who finished seventeenth or whatever in the Tour. In Colombia, we say, 'Eighth and eightieth are the same.' I had a job to do: to ride to Col de la Ramaz until I couldn't do what I was doing in the first kilometres, and then, boom! – peel off the front and save energy for the next day. But on the Col de la Ramaz, when I began to drop off the pace, Johan said, 'OK, Victor, relax. Wait for the *gruppetto*.' He didn't have to say it. I've never wanted to hang on to arrive three or five minutes down, with an eye on the general classification, hoping to hear, 'Hey, Victor, you arrived tenth, you were only three minutes down,' because they're not going to say that. They're going to say, 'Victor, if you saved that much energy, you weren't riding hard enough,' because to come tenth you need a lot of energy. They'll say, 'He doesn't work honestly.' In any case, wherever you finish today, you pay for tomorrow. So I lost the jersey. It was a beautiful reign, and I enjoyed every minute, but my first thought was, *Finally, I'm going to be able to sleep*. The weight of the world had been taken off my shoulders. I wouldn't have changed the day I lost the jersey for anything. I just wanted to sleep.

General Classification after stage 7: Lyon–Morzine-Avoriaz
Total distance: 1272.5 km
Leader's time: 29 hrs 10 mins 39 secs
Leader's average speed: 43.603 kph

1	VIRENQUE Richard	Quick Step-Davitamon	119	FRA	
2	ARMSTRONG Lance	US Postal-Berry Floor	1	USA	2 mins 37
3	ALDAG Rolf	Team Telekom	23	GER	2 mins 48
4	RUBIERA José Luis	US Postal-Berry Floor	9	ESP	2 mins 59
5	HERAS Roberto	US Postal-Berry Floor	2	ESP	3 mins 3
6	BELOKI Joseba	ONCE-Eroski	11	ESP	3 mins 9
7	JAKSCHE Jörg	ONCE-Eroski	15	GER	3 mins 14
8	BELTRÁN Manolo	US Postal-Berry Floor	3	ESP	3 mins 15
9	ULLRICH Jan	Team Bianchi	131	GER	3 mins 15
10	AZEVEDO José	ONCE-Eroski	13	POR	3 mins 37
103	PEÑA Victor Hugo	US Postal-Berry Floor	8	COL	23 mins 26

Borders and
Border Crossings

If a modern committee sat down to design the showpiece stage race of world cycling, it would bear little resemblance to the Tour de France. It would have no national home, which would mean no set-piece mountain stages over the Izoard and the Tourmalet, or sprint finishes at Bordeaux and Paris, and no nostalgic comparisons with past performances, and it would probably not even be three weeks long: the Tour's duration and itinerary are a product of history. This new, rational Tour would be context-free, placeless. And the Tour de France is anything but that. In short, it would have a completely different meaning. And the Tour de France *has* meaning.

Between Waterloo and the Western Front, Europe experienced an extended period of relative peace. It was an era of scientific discovery, opened by Faraday and closed by Einstein. In between, Doppler and Darwin, Mendel (the founder of genetic science) and Mendeleyev (the periodic table), Edison (inventor of the light bulb) and Rutherford (who discovered the atomic nucleus) changed the future. In France, Foucault, Pasteur, the Curies, and Nobel laureates Becquerel (Physics,

1903), Moissan (Chemistry, 1906) and Laveran (Medicine, 1907) transformed mankind's understanding of the world. It was also an age of invention, yielding the first plastics and synthetic fibres, linoleum and the zip fastener, Linus Yale's first lock and King Gillette's first disposable safety razor, and altered communications for ever thanks to celluloid, the telephone, the gramophone, photography, Lewis Waterman's first fat fountain pens, camera film in rolls, wireless telegraphy, the internal-combustion engine, the motorcar and the aeroplane. Frenchmen developed the first successful airship, the gyroscope, open-hearth steel production, the first commercial electric generator, the zinc-carbon battery, artificial silk and the cinematograph. Science and invention, funded by the exploitation of industrial labour at home and colonial rule abroad, powered a social revolution. The industrial bourgeoisie, that phalanx of industrialists, merchants, bankers, lawyers and bureaucrats, transformed each scientific advance into life-changing products for the general populace and fantastic wealth for the tiny minority. Across the Atlantic, steel made magnates of John D. Rockefeller and Andrew Carnegie. In France, it propelled Eugène and Adolphe Schneider, two sons of a modest provincial notary, into the stratosphere (another French discovery) of the super-rich. The emergence of great retail outlets extended both the upper reaches of the bourgeoisie – Aristide Boucicaut, the son of a lowly hatter, founded the Parisian department store Le Bon Marché and was worth twenty-two million francs at his death in 1877 – and its lower divisions by demanding of working-class sales clerks not just stock phrases but the mindset of courtesy and self-restraint in which the middle classes had trained themselves.

The bicycle was part of this great groundswell of the

Western bourgeoisie. So too were the journalist-creators of the first cycle races – Lesclide, Martin, Giffard and Desgrange – energetic achievers who considered regulated desire essential to the formation of good character, preached the subjugation of animal urges into productive respectability and idealised the self-made man who conquers his world without inherited wealth, advanced education and distinguished forebears. The early road racers must have embodied these values with startling literalism: working men who, in the years of Taylor's first time-and-motion studies and Ford's first production lines, pedalled through the night without even a freewheel that would allow them a moment's respite. The twelve thousand francs the former child sweep Maurice Garin earned winning the first Tour de France were six times a working man's annual wage. A few years later, Octave Lapize's father calculated that his profoundly deaf son had earned twenty times a working man's annual wage by winning the 1909 Paris–Roubaix. In the great age of the Blue Riband and the burgeoning Manhattan skyline, the racing cyclist was as much an icon of his age as the ocean-going liner and the skyscraper. In 1913, the Futurist painter Umberto Boccioni, who celebrated speeding trains and motorcars, portrayed *The Dynamism of a Cyclist*, and the Cubist Jean Metzinger depicted the winner of Paris–Roubaix. Little wonder: Garin's 1903 average of 26.450 kilometres per hour over two and a half thousand kilometres was reportedly faster than the trains of the time. If cycling was compatible with this dream of speed, it staved off the nightmare visions of mental and physical degeneration that haunted psychiatry, criminology and a number of social commentaries and debates, best illustrated by H.G. Wells' *The Time Machine*. And if the bourgeois devotion to numbers, timetables and fussy punctuality also had the power to imprison, cycling responded to that, too, with its ambiguous cocktail of restlessness and rigidity.

As the most modern and accessible means of transport of its age, the bicycle was part of a wider time-and-motion revolution powered by the national railway networks, World Standard Time, wireless telegraphy (invented in 1894) and the telephone (1876). Years after the 1884 Prime Meridian Conference in Washington had established Greenwich as the zero meridian and divided the earth into time zones, France's system of time-keeping was the most chaotic in Western Europe: the local hour was still fixed according to solar readings or to astronomical time taken from fixed stars, official Paris time was exactly nine minutes and twenty-one seconds ahead of Greenwich, and the railways ran five minutes behind Paris time to give passengers extra time to board. Paris time became legal national time as late as 1891; President Poincaré made up for lost time hosting the 1912 International Conference on time signals; on the morning of 1 July 1913, the Eiffel Tower transmitted the first time signal around the world. By then, the Tour de France, which started and finished in Paris until 1947, had been performing the same function nationally for a decade, passing through the regions like a regal entourage, connecting them to the capital with the invisible lines it traced over the nation, bringing Paris time and modernity to the regions.

To Parisians, the immense landscapes and mind-boggling distances covered by the early cycle races must have been the perfect panacea to the enclosure of daily life that had begun at the midpoint of the nineteenth century, when Napoleon III and his prefect, Georges Haussmann, began to remodel the city. Before the municipal makeover known as Haussmannisation, Paris had been a city of apartment houses with ground-floor shops, imposing entrances supervised by porters, and residential apartments above. Street life continued on public landings floored with the same concrete, stone or marble used in the streets they closely resembled. Haussmann confined hitherto open sites. Street carnivals entered dance halls. Artisans and mechanics were driven into workshops. The open market at Les Halles was covered. Women who had laundered clothes on the banks of the Seine were provided with purpose-built *lavoirs*. Interior floors began to be of wood; new zoning practices isolated residential neighbourhoods from businesses, separating domestic and commercial spaces, interior and exterior, and endorsing bourgeois privacy with an architectural programme. If Haussmann's urban revolution resulted in a sense of spatial constriction, cycle racing's response was a stunning encounter with the open landscape, an encounter that also connected seamlessly with a European-wide re-evaluation of the countryside that in England saw the establishment of the National Trust in 1895 to safeguard sites of historic interest or natural beauty, and a 1907 act empowering it to hold them in trust for the nation, and in Germany to the foundation of the Dürerbund in 1903, and a year later the Heimatschutz, created to protect historical monuments and natural areas. In France, the Touring Club de France, founded in 1892 by seven cyclists, and the Automobile Club de France, founded in 1895 by de Dion and associates, devoted themselves to opening the magnificence of the French countryside to the touring public, much as television coverage of the modern Tour does today. The former was responsible for the construction of the *Route des Grandes Alpes*, the latter for the *Route Thermale du Touring Club de France* through the Pyrenees. Both are at the heart of the Tour de France's mountain itineraries.

Its pioneers regarded the bicycle as more than an affordable means of mobility; it was an engine of improvement, a vehicle of an almost Messianic optimism, yet it coexisted with something darker. Between 1789 and 1914 France went through two empires, a monarchy, two short-lived republics and a third that faltered for years. Frenchmen had been killing Frenchmen on barricades or in government-backed shootings from the Revolutionary Terror to the *semaine sanglante* – the week of blood – that followed the collapse of the Paris Commune in May 1871. The loss of Alsace-Lorraine following the siege of Paris and defeat in the Franco-Prussian War had left an open wound that would not close until after the First World War and the repatriation of the lost territories, while in the 1890s the depth of bigotry in an otherwise civilised country revealed by the Dreyfus affair only added to a sense of national dislocation. If cycling races yielded an emotional return that was greater than the local inconvenience they caused, was it that the French gained some veiled psychic fulfilment from the completion, in emotional scenes of triumph, of arduous athletic odysseys across their land? A century or more ago, the French pioneers organised their races as much to develop French muscle as to boost the cycling industry. Deeply affected by the French defeat in the 1870 Franco-Prussian War, they believed that the bicycle could play a part in reclaiming Alsace-Lorraine. If the first cycle races expressed the shock of defeat in the Franco-Prussian War and the loss of Alsace-Lorraine, they did so unsatisfactorily. Perhaps it took the Tour de France, the last and greatest of these expressions, to expiate France's national distress and transcend it – despite the fact that the first two Tours, identical, save for minor junction changes that shortened the 1904 route by thirty-one kilometres, were little more than circuits around the Massif

Central. The eleven-stage itinerary of the 1905 race entirely effaced those beginnings and spread the race over a far greater extension of France, adding 500 kilometres to the total distance. By the inclusion of Lille, Nice and Brest in 1906 and Perpignan and Luchon in 1910, the notion that the Tour should police France's borders gradually emerged. By visiting Metz four times between 1907 and 1910 and claiming German-occupied Lothringen for its own, Henri Desgrange began to foster the Tour's geopolitical potential. By stopping at Cherbourg on Normandy's Cotentin Peninsula and Le Havre on the Alabaster Coast, the 1911 Tour incorporated the north coast into its geography. With the addition of mountain stages through the Pyrenees in 1910 and the Alps in 1911, and the integration of liberated Alsace-Lorraine in 1919, Desgrange completed a model that would serve until the late 1930s, when the Tour visited the regional capitals: 'Strasbourg! Metz!' he rhapsodised, 'and it isn't a dream! . . . I cannot resist recalling our first Tour de France in 1903 with its ridiculously small itinerary: Lyon, Marseille, Toulouse, Bordeaux, Nantes, Paris . . . With Strasbourg and Metz, our ambitions are fulfilled; the Tour de France is complete.' The Tours de France of the 1920s and early 1930s kept to the borders; the continuous line they drew around France formed a protective circle more complete and more psychically engaging than the Maginot Line would achieve.

The density and complexity of the French road infra-structure, and the social acceptability of the Tour, which allows its designers a wide range of choice, may make it possible to read the Tour itinerary, year by year, for traces of a dialogue with the world beyond, as if the Tour de France itself were an elaborate piece of street art daubed on the roads of France and deserving of the same critical attention as

Boccioni or Metzinger. If the Tour had expressed only (*only!*) the psychic aftershock of the Franco-Prussian War, it would have ceased to exist by 1919. Certainly, hostilities between Prussia and a France still ruled by parliamentary monarchy seem of little consequence as the US Postal armada shepherds Lance Armstrong towards the Tourmalet. Yet the Tour has assumed many meanings during its history. The introduction of the yellow jersey in 1919 has been described as a sign of rebirth, the colour of the sun, illuminating the post-war austerity. This, and the virulent eruptions of nationalism in Italy, Germany and Spain, no doubt reinforced the relevance of the Tour as a defensive symbol during the 1920s and 1930s.

Until 1912, every Tour followed a clockwise itinerary around France; in 1913, Desgrange made a radical innovation by creating the anticlockwise Tour, which he developed each year until 1932. In 1933, he reverted to a clockwise loop, which characterised eight of the nine Tours between then and 1947. In the mid-1930s, the Tour actively began to seek out novelty. Perhaps the completeness lacked a corresponding sense of inclusion – a sense reflected in the 1936 election of France's first socialist government under Léon Blum. Where the 1934 route included twenty-four stages or semi-stages (two or three short stages in a day) and no new stage towns, 1935 expanded into twenty-seven stages or semi-stages, with one new stage town (Rochefort-sur-Mer). The year 1936 saw twenty-seven stages or semi-stages and three new stage towns (Saintes, Chôlet and Vire), while 1937 grew even more unwieldy with thirty-one stages or semi-stages and four new towns (Lons-le-Saunier, Champagnole, Bourg-Madame and Royan). The anticlockwise 1938 route was a hybrid of the previous year's (clockwise) Tour and the previous anticlockwise Tour in 1932. In place of the annual anxiety to be comprehensive, it acknowledged for the first time that each Tour can make its own emphases. In the course of twenty-nine stages/semi-stages it excised Finisterre in the extreme north-west from the Tour, instead visiting three entirely new towns in the north-east: Reims, Laon and Saint-Quentin. The following year, the Tour returned to the extreme north-west by visiting Brest, took :n two new stage towns of St Raphael and Monaco before entering the Alps, and three more new towns – Bonneval, Bourg-St Maurice and Annecy – before leaving them. Then, omitting the north-east entirely, it cut across country from Dôle and Dijon to Troyes and Paris. The 1939 Tour also included a mountain time trial for the first time. This sudden taste for the new in stage towns and types and routes across the interior suggests that the Tour's relationship with the geography of France was entering a new phase even before the outbreak of the Second World War and Henri Desgrange's death on 16 August 1940 made change inevitable.

The Jacques Goddet era officially started in 1947, although the Tour had been changing in the 1930s, and the 1938 and 1939 Tours exhibit the tastes of Desgrange's successor. However, an abyss lay between the pre- and post-war Tours. Desgrange had experimented warily; Goddet was easily bored. After 1938, in the ideology of the Tour itinerary, the recent past became less a blueprint to elaborate on than a model to react against or compensate for. Borders became limits not to police but to cross; hinterlands were no longer for circumnavigating, but for exploring. Unlike our hypothetical Tour planned by a technical committee, Goddet's routes were studies in self-quotation in which every act of victory or defeat opened a dialogue with the past. The continuous lines of the Desgrange era contrast starkly with the repeated, brutal interruptions of history marked by two world wars in three decades. Goddet the alchemist was happy to blend whatever flavours the world had to offer. He designed his first Tour in 1947, and it was a virtuoso demonstration of expertise in the tradition Desgrange had created. The Tour started and finished in Paris. Its twenty-one stages and no semi-stages were a departure from late Desgrange; between 1934 and 1939, semi-stages effectively raised the number of stages to twenty-seven or more, making recovery almost impossible for the riders. Stages two (Lille to Brussels) and three (Brussels to Luxembourg) show Goddet's sense of European identity. The foreign excursion gave a radical look to the route, although the Tour as a whole is traditional by comparison with 1938 and 1939. Desgrange's cherished Strasbourg was a tribute to his master, while Lyon was a back reference to the earliest Tours, and therefore to Géo Lefèvre and the first Tour de France winner Maurice Garin (in 1903 and 1904, Garin had been the first to cross the finish line at Lyon; in 1908, 1909 and 1910, Luxembourg's François Faber, the first non-French winner of the Tour, won the Lyon stage). Stage seven of the 1947 Tour was held between Lyon and Grenoble, a route last used between 1908 and 1910. In two of those years, the stage was won by the eventual Tour champion: Faber in 1909, and Lapize in 1910. Stages eight, nine and ten visited the stage towns Grenoble, Briançon, Digne and Nice, replicating a sequence from Desgrange's 1936 and 1937 itineraries. The start and finish towns of stages ten, eleven and twelve belonged to the string Nice-Cannes-Marseille-Nîmes-Montpellier, which in one permutation or other was a constant between 1930 and 1938. Where Desgrange traditionally visited Béziers, Narbonne or Perpignan, Goddet stopped at Carcassonne for the first time in Tour history. The stage from Luchon to Pau is a post-1930 innovation; the chain Luchon-

Pau-Bordeaux was used in 1932, 1935, 1936 and 1937 as a variant on Luchon-Bayonne-Bordeaux (1925–29). Les Sables d'Olonne means 1919 to 1931; the resort had replaced La Rochelle as the Tour's Atlantic stronghold, just as La Rochelle had supplanted Nantes in 1911. Furthermore, the stage Les Sables d'Olonne to Vannes recalls 1925 and 1927–31, when Brest was always the next stop. St-Brieuc means 1938, interchangeable with Vire or Rennes on the way to Caen, the northwest gateway to and from Paris between 1905 and 1910, before being replaced by Le Havre from 1911 to 1925, and returning to favour for the years 1928–39. Goddet's play of quotation and variation, tradition and innovation, yielded a classic race settled only on the final stage, when Jean Robic, a tempestuous Breton who rode in a leather helmet, attacked on the Bonsecours climb just outside Rouen and won the Tour of the Liberation on the final stage for a regional team representing West France without ever having worn the yellow jersey. Where Desgrange transplanted entire limbs from one Tour to the next, Goddet inserted tiny segments of the race's DNA into entirely new contexts.

Before the creation of the European Community, Goddet was supplementing border-hugging routes in the Desgrange tradition with excursions into Italy, Switzerland and Belgium (in 1948) or Belgium, Spain and Italy (1949), and adding smaller regional settlements to the established stage towns. His first major innovation was to advance inland from the Atlantic coast in 1950 by visiting Angers (for the second time in Tour history) and Niort (for the first), and then to venture east of the Rhône and into central France, visiting St-Étienne. Despite crowd trouble, causing the Italian team, including the yellow jersey, to withdraw and Goddet to replace the scheduled visit to San Remo with an impromptu stop at

Menton, the new tendency to explore inland France was confirmed in the following years.

The major transformation of 1951 was the desertion of Paris as the host of the race start. Until 1950, every Tour had traced a complete loop starting and ending in Paris, like a royal procession, taking a taste of the capital to the provinces, then returning symbolically from the nation's periphery to its centre. The proof of the importance of this order of centre and periphery to Desgrange lies in the 1926 Tour, when he sought a solution to the ennui of the long, essentially flat stages that inevitably led from the mountains to the race finish in Paris. By moving the race start to Évian, he allowed the race to complete its loop with a mountain stage ending at Évian before riding back to Paris in just two stages. The record books accordingly commemorate the 1926 Tour as the first to start outside Paris. Not so: the event started with a ceremonial prologue in which the riders, bike-bound but in casual clothes, rolled down from the Arc de Triomphe, along the Champs-Élysées to the Gare de Lyon, where they joined the Évian train. Desgrange needed his Paris start. Even after 1950, it took time for Goddet to abandon the Paris start completely. The 1951 Tour (anticlockwise) started in Metz, border-crossed to Gand, before entering Paris at the end of stage four. The stage five start gave the capital its chance to seal the race with its approval, and allowed the route to start the time-honoured closed loop. In 1951, however, Goddet's innovation became definitive: since then, the Tour has only started in Paris to celebrate its fiftieth edition in 1963 and its centenary in 2003. The 1958, 1961 and 1971 Tours resembled 1951, with early stages speeding towards the Île de France before being diverted into the loop of a noose; the 1986 Tour started in the Paris *banlieue* of Boulogne-Billancourt.

The Tour had always mediated between national and local identity. By abandoning the Paris start, Goddet's Tour became a barometer of French decentralisation, long held back by the perceived need to concentrate power in response to external threats, and a persistent idea in France that central government requires the maximum of powers. The twenty-two regions of France were created in June 1955; the regional planning authorities – Datar (Délégation à l'aménagement du territoire et de l'action régionale) and the regional prefects – were established in 1963 and 1964 respectively. Bordeaux, Lille, Lyon and Strasbourg were recognised as urban communes in 1966. General de Gaulle's decentralising instincts led to his political demise when his proposals to give the regions considerable powers over departments, ascribe a special status to Corsica and modify the Constitution met with opposition from the Senate, which faced reform, and were rejected in a 1969 referendum. By the time the first great decentralisation and regionalisation laws were passed between March 1982 and March 1983, the Tour de France had been exploring France's interior for three decades.

The great assemblies that congregate in the Tour towns are rare in the faraway places of nations, allowing little-known localities to enter national and international awareness. Local and regional newspapers that waste few resources covering the FIFA World Cup or the Olympic Games fill pages with race information and local stories surrounding the coming of the Tour. Their language differs from that of the national and international press, by virtue of local knowledge. The destination of the first long individual time trial of the 2003 race, Cap' Découverte, is an activity holiday centre built over a disused opencast mine. The Tarn-Albi edition of the newspaper *La Dépêche du Midi* snubbed the appellation Cap'

Découverte employed by the official Tour map and literature, substituting the name of a nearby village, Blaye-les-Mines, while even the national press and official Tour information were torn between referring to the stage finish of the first Pyrenean stage by its commercial designation Ax-3 Domaines, or using the uninflected local toponym Plateau de Bonascre. It is too strong to describe these discrepancies as a power struggle, but only occupiers change local nomenclature, and the Paris-based Société du Tour de France comes as an outsider.

As new roads were driven into the Alps and Pyrenees, the Tour penetrated deeper into the mountains. New routes allowed the first finishes at Alpe d'Huez, Sestriere and the Puy-de-Dôme. The pass over the Col d'Iseran in 1938 took the Tour as high as Europe's roads allowed. Goddet was indulging his taste for new types of obstacle as well as new types of itinerary. Under Desgrange, no Tour had started outside the capital, let alone outside France. In 1954, Goddet allowed Amsterdam to host the first foreign start. In 1958 the Tour began in Brussels. After just one foreign start in the 1960s (at Cologne in 1965), the Tour has started abroad three times per decade ever since (in the 1970s starting from Le Haye [1973], Charleroi [1975] and Leyde [1978]; in the 1980s, Frankfurt [1980], Basel [1982] and West Berlin [1987]; and in the 1990s, San Sebastian [1992], s'Hertogenbosch [1996] and Dublin [1998]).

At the stage start at Basel in 1982, Goddet composed an editorial for *L'Équipe* that became known as the Basel Appeal. Inspired by the success of the 1982 FIFA World Cup, which he called 'the greatest televised show on Earth', Goddet made a series of proposals for the future of the Tour de France: every four years, following the rhythm of the Olympic Games and the FIFA World Cup, and specifically, the year after the

Olympic Games, a globalised Tour de France should be held. The itinerary, he argued, should touch the greatest number of nations as possible, while keeping the route, in its majority, in France. Goddet's fantasy route was a race start and two stages in a location to be decided each time, followed by stages in the USA, Great Britain, Holland, Belgium, Luxembourg, Germany, Switzerland, Italy, Monaco, Spain, and nine stages in France, including the race finish on the Champs-Élysées. Although his proposal is unfeasible – it would be impossible to hold a stage every day and allow the riders time to recover – Goddet suggested something similar for the itinerary of the 2003 Centenary Tour. In a Paris restaurant in 1997, Goddet proposed not a Tour de France, but a Tour of the World including several days of racing around New York or Moscow, with many hours of flying to reach the other great capitals of the world, before finishing on the Champs-Élysées.

Jean-Marie Leblanc humoured him, but ignored him: the Tour de France has never needed unrealistic flights of fantasy to achieve globalisation. The 2003 Tour route had no gimmicks, beyond visiting the 1903 Tour towns of Lyon, Marseille, Toulouse, Bordeaux, Nantes and Paris, and offering a special Centennial Prize to the rider who consistently placed the highest on those stages. Where Desgrange's Tours described a continuous loop over France, earning the Tour the soubriquet of *la grande boucle*, Goddet's traced an increasingly discontinuous spiral. From 1962, the unstable relationship between Goddet and Lévitan produced itineraries consisting of broken segments and spirals, especially in the early 1970s and 1980s. The 1982 route could be described as a series of anticlockwise segments followed by two clockwise knots. It was a trend that Jean-Marie Leblanc inherited, although he tempered it with his inherent sense of moderation. After all, in the 1970s the routes of the Tour de France and other major races had been rife with same-day semi-stages, late finishes, early starts, and energy-sapping transfers between stage finishes and stage starts. With less time to sleep and recover, the riders had interrupted the Paris–Nice stage race in 1977 with strike action. More would affect the 1978 Tour de France. As an ex-rider, a leading cycling journalist in the 1970s, and a man who considered consensus as the best solution of conflicting interests, Leblanc recognised that the race director is not always free to follow his whims.

The first Tour Leblanc designed took place almost entirely within France, crossing the border only once to reach Geneva, Desgrange's sole foreign town (excepting German-occupied Metz). The itinerary of the 1990 Tour, with its stops at Sarrebourg and Épinal in the north-east, the chain of stages connecting the Alps to the Pyrenees via Villard de Lans, St-Étienne, Millau, Revel and Luz-Ardiden, and the final week encompassing Pau, Bordeaux, Limoges and a time trial around Lac de Vassivière in the Limousin, strongly evoked the 1985 edition – the last Tour won by a Frenchman (and Leblanc would return to a similar layout in 1995). The race started at Futuroscope, an unfinished tourist attraction near Poitier in which the Tour umbrella company, ASO, had a financial interest. Bearing in mind that the Tour had regularly run at a deficit between 1947 and 1987 and had to be bailed out by its sponsors, the newspapers *L'Équipe* and *Le Parisien Libéré*, Leblanc's first Tour had consolidation written all over it. He included just two transfers for the riders, where 1989 had seen three, 1988 four and 1987 five. Otherwise, the itinerary demonstrated his adherence to the Goddet-Lévitan tradition, with one distinction: where the rebellious Goddet had marked his first Tour by taking it to the picturesque Cathar stronghold of Carcassonne for the first time, Leblanc, a devout Catholic, celebrated his accession with a stage finish beneath the towering island monastery of Mont St Michel.

In Goddet's footsteps, Leblanc has described it as 'the vocation of the Tour de France to inspire with new vigour corners of France too often forgotten'. On Bastille Day 1995, the Tour visited Mende, the capital of the Lozère, France's least densely populated department, whose population had been diminishing for two centuries. The Tour organisers let it be known that the stage was a response to the decentralisation debate of 1993 and 1994, which had resulted in the February 1995 Pasqua reforms. The choice was rewarded with a brilliant stage win from France's finest rider, Laurent Jalabert, at the end of a 198-kilometre breakaway.

So European has the Tour become that just five editions have remained wholly within France since the Second World War. Of the twenty-six Tours de France that haven't crossed France's borders, twenty were the creations of Lefèvre and Desgrange, five belong to the Goddet-Lévitan era, and just one was designed by Leblanc: our Tour, the Centenary Tour in 2003. And it was as if the centenary route itself was willing Armstrong to win his fifth title, for despite the fact that clockwise Tours are in the clear minority, the four riders before Lance Armstrong to win five times all completed the feat by winning a clockwise Tour.

The internationalisation of the Tour route does not directly parallel the creation of the European institutions or the various phases of European Union expansion. Internationalisation has never embraced the wider francophone world, the more than twenty-five nations in which French is an official language, or the fifty-five member states of the International Organisation for Francophonie. In 1999, the Tour organisers took over the Tour de Burkina Faso, and from that beginning, perhaps francophone Africa may enter cycling history. The question remains whether the post-War fascination with discontinuous routes reflects anything more than a desire to explore more and different regions of France, and the need to pass through photogenic backdrops to meet the demands of television coverage. Is the Tour itinerary the mute product of interactions between town administrations and the Tour organisers, or does it have expressive powers of its own? If so, does it merely express the tastes of its director, or does it encode transformations in the underlying means of economic production in France? What can be said with some certainty is that the Tour de France is a voice in a dense cultural dialogue in which its post-war discontinuities echo not just the discontinuities of twentieth-century history, fractured by two World Wars and post-colonial turmoil, but the fascination in the art, literature and philosophy of post-war France – the post-war world – with the non-linear, the undecidable and discontinuities of all types.

The First Long Climb

Monday 21 July 2003, 13:15: 2 kilometres before Montastruc

Chavanel and Botero have nearly a minute on us. They'll complete the intermediate sprint together and share the points without celebration. When we approach the sprint, a trio of riders races past me. Australia's Stuart O'Grady leads out his Norwegian team-mate Thor Hushovd, with another Australian, Baden Cooke, the category leader, on their heels. Cooke swings out of Hushovd's slipstream and passes him. Too early: the Norwegian comes back and beats him to the line – an explosion of energy worth just two sprint points, and as many bonus seconds, to the winner. They are several hundred metres ahead of us, but we let them go. Even working together, such heavy physiques won't get far into the mountains. The front of the peloton is blue: five US Postal Service riders – me, Ekimov, Padrnos, Landis and Hincapie – open the way for Armstrong. Heras is collecting water bottles from the team car. Chechu is drafting behind Lance, protecting his rear wheel and conserving energy for the final climb. Beltrán is behind him, the team's smallest rider casting the weakest slipstream. He offers little protection to the great frame of Jan

Ullrich, who follows him with his domestiques Félix García Casas, Aitor Garmendia and Fabrizio Guidi. Alexander Vinokourov is in Guidi's slipstream, followed by his team-mates Giuseppe Guerini, Erik Zabel and Daniele Nardello.

We are the only team fully kitted out with the new ten-speed Shimano groupset. On the other Shimano teams, only three or four riders are using it. We have the best equipment, as well as the best riders, although even the best equipment isn't foolproof. On the Côte de Castelbajac, the last fourth-category climb of the day, George Hincapie loses his chain. Lance reaches out and pushes him, but George drops back through the field. Stéphane Goubert of Jean Delatour and Alexander Bocharov of AG2R attack on the climb, taking Commesso and Cédric Vasseur of Cofidis with them. We close them down. Goubert crosses four or five seconds ahead of me, but gets no further. Then George reaches the front of the peloton. Eki greets him with a pat on the back and he slots into the second position. As we enter the village of Houeydets, yet another AG2R rider, Iñigo Chaurreau, a Basque with a French surname, flares away from the peloton. When he has a small advantage, he flicks his arm, the signal to ask the rider on his wheel to take a turn at the front – perhaps it's only then that he realises he's alone. We don't react. There's another intermediate sprint in twenty-five kilometres. If the sprinters want another fight for third place, their teams will have to come to the front and chase Chaurreau. Then, still in Houeydets, four riders, led by Stuart O'Grady, launch another violent attack. I rise out of the saddle and lift the pace; it takes no more than thirty seconds to neutralise the move. Seconds later, another attack shoots past: O'Grady again, with Flickinger and Julian Usano among them. This time, it takes us seventy seconds to snuff them out.

Lannemezan is the last landmark before we roll out on to the plain that leads to the foot of the Col d'Aspin. Chaurreau is still ten seconds ahead of us. We relax the pace to allow him to disappear. The front of the peloton consists of Ekimov, Padrnos, Rubiera, me, George, Lance, Landis and Beltrán. South of Lannemezan, we go over a motorway bridge and the rhythm eases again. Several riders stop at the side of the road. Others perform the same function from the saddle. As the protected riders and their mountain domestiques take on liquid and solid food – high-energy bars and gels washed down with sports drinks – the breakaway riders will be working hard to extend their lead. It's just before two o'clock. Two Saeco riders, Fabio Sacchi and Paolo Fornaciari, slot into the US Postal line at the front of the race, helping with the pace; a third, Salvatore Commesso, is riding beside Lance. I don't know why they're there. Neither of the Saeco leaders, Simoni and Di Luca, is strong enough to attack today. Perhaps Italian television coverage starts at two, and the team wants to put riders where the cameras will see them. Minutes later, I hear over the radio that Chaurreau is one minute fifty seconds ahead of us, and Chavanel and Botero at four minutes thirty. The Saeco riders are still in the line, riding *tempo*. Twelve kilometres and eight minutes later, Chaurreau is two minutes forty ahead, with Chavanel and Botero six minutes twenty.

The road runs beside a river and a railway line, cutting parallel routes across the plain as the hills rise to either side. Ahead, the mountains rise unseen through the haze. In the hypnotic afternoon, we close in on the Col d'Aspin. We haven't ridden it this year. We only trained on the stages we didn't know: the stage to Gap, and the final Pyrenean stage from Pau to Bayonne. On the descent from the Col d'Izoard, I fell;

thankfully I was unhurt. We rode the Col de la Ramaz during the Dauphiné Libéré, so we didn't train there. The Col d'Aspin was part of our preparation for the 2001 Tour. We rode in repetitions of five hundred metres at fifty pedal-turns per minute, followed by a kilometre at ninety. As we began to climb, Armstrong said, 'Not here, it's too easy. Further up' – he knows exactly where the steepest stretches are on each climb. The passes that cross the Pyrenees are marked by kilometre signs that give the gradient and the distance from the col. That day I committed the Aspin to memory: the steep start, the long shallow climb, then right and left, and right and left again, into the wind on each right-hand section, out of it as you roll left, then into it again, then out. In 2001, I rode the Aspin at the front, looking for my father. It turned out he was right at the top, so I led for the entire climb. This morning, Johan told me to remember that day. As we approach, I'm apprehensive. After so many kilometres riding hard on the flat, I don't know how my body will react: climbing is a different effort using different muscles. The riders begin to get nervous and look for position as we near the pass. The crowds thicken, clapping inflatable tubes and huge green hands – handouts from the publicity caravan – and we swing slowly around a sharp right-hand bend. Suddenly, we are ascending. Botero and Chavanel turned this corner eight minutes ago; Chaurreau was four minutes twenty behind them. I think to myself, *We'll just have to see.* I'm afraid I'm going to drop back, when I hear over my shoulder, 'Slower. Take it easy.' The valley drops away smoothly. The sun is shining strongly for the first time that day. I dowse myself in water, and drink not deeply but often: keep the body core cool.

There are plenty of flags. Brittany, Catalunya, the Basque

irrukiña. Beneath the flag of Asturias, the yellow cross on blue, we pass Rubiera's family. I nod my head to the right and Ekimov takes over. Ullrich has stopped to change a wheel. Pavel is leading the peloton; he's the best climber of the bigger riders. When I ride behind him, I don't recover much. I prefer to be at the front at my own pace, so I take over. Everyone is looking at everyone else, assessing each others' strength. Armstrong is some way behind us, riding in the body of the group, perhaps pretending, perhaps not, that he's in poor shape. Behind the peloton, Aitor Garmendia and Angel Casero are leading Ullrich back to the peloton. Each time we move into the wind, we form an echelon, a diagonal line across the road. Despite the airstream, I'm sweating heavily. Botero and Chavanel eke seconds from the gradient. With seven kilometres of the Aspin to climb, we're nine minutes ten seconds behind Botero and Chavanel. With five to go, we're nine minutes twenty-five behind. Chaurreau is nearly six minutes behind them, alone in no man's land. There are still four US Postal riders at the front of the peloton. Michael Boogerd is just behind us. Gilberto Simoni, who started the attacks with him this morning, has dropped behind. Alberto López de Munaín, a Euskaltel-Euskadi rider, overtakes me and rides at the front. As he comes past, I say, 'Alberto, take it easy.' But we ride the final three kilometres faster. 'Easy, Alberto.' As we approach the summit, we're surrounded by crowds calling for Richard Virenque and the Basques. Virenque, Laurent Dufaux and Christophe Moreau move forward to contest the mountain prize. Virenque darts out as we reach the summit and takes the points for fourth place with Laurent Dufaux, his close friend but also the only rider who can mathematically take the jersey from him, on his wheel. Providing he completes the Tour, Virenque will now win the polka-dot jersey. Then we start the descent, whipping around the bends and plummeting into the valley. I like to ride behind Lance because I'm afraid of moving my bike slightly to check something, or misjudging a curve, and bringing him down. When we're training, I like to take it easy on the descents because of traffic. Lance takes them at full speed, rehearsing the corners.

It takes just fifteen minutes to reach the feed zone at Sainte-Marie-de-Campan, the little town at the foot of the Aspin's west face, thirteen kilometres from the col. As the road levels out, Commesso rides past me, then pulls over to the side of the road to piss from the saddle. Lance does the same behind me. The peloton coasts as the yellow jersey rejoins the group. Seven US Postal riders lead Lance into Sainte-Marie-de-Campan, over ten minutes behind Chavanel and Botero. The next thing we hear in our earpieces is that Chavanel has dropped Botero. We collect our *musettes* and transfer the contents into our pockets or straight into our mouths. At the foot of the Tourmalet, two Euskaltel-Euskadi riders, Iñigo Landaluze and Mikel Artetxe, move just ahead of me at the front of the main peloton. We ride even faster after collecting our feedbags, because the Euskadi guys raise the pace. Roberto Heras is labouring in the group with Pavel. With nine kilometres still to climb, Botero is a minute and a half behind Chavanel. Then comes Chaurreau, five and a half minutes later, and the peloton another six minutes back. We pass through La Mongie, the halfway point on the climb. Mikel Artetxe is still ahead of me. I whisper to him, 'Take it easy, Mikel, recuperate, catch your breath, Mikel, relax, so that I can catch mine.' Three Bianchi riders are poised at my wheel. Lance is still not among the leading twenty riders. He's playing mind games with Ullrich and Vinokourov. Artetxe imposes another acceleration. This time, Pavel and Eki drop off the pace. Only Triki and Floyd are behind me now. Then Floyd drops off the pace. I'm strangely comfortable, inured to the stresses of the ascent. But soon, I know, the sound and dash and blur will return and I'll slide back into the pain and then drift backwards through the group.

La Mongie, the halfway point on the Tourmalet. Bourg d'Oisans, the start of Alpe d'Huez. Only the place names that mark strategic points have some meaning to us. The other hundreds of towns and villages we pass mean little to us. I imagine the French riders know the places we go through, but the rest of us live in an abstraction. We rarely see the race route on a conventional map: it only exists as an altimetric profile. The landscapes we ride through are our workplace, level corridors and rising stairways like an office block. The horizontal kilometres channel us from one climb to the next. For instance, the top of the Col d'Aspin is kilometre ninety-four of the stage. There are sixty-five and a half kilometres to go. But I look at it like this: there's a fifteen-and-a-half-kilometre climb up the Tourmalet, followed by another seventeen-kilometre climb up to Luz-Ardiden, so I've really got thirty-two and a half kilometres left. The flat sections and descents don't count. The mountain stages don't frighten me, because I think, *This part is descending, that part is flat, and the hard bit is this small section*. If I have thirty kilometres of suffering, I remember that in Colombia there are eighty-kilometre climbs. So although we ride on the public roads, and go through places everyone goes through, and see features everyone else sees, we inhabit a different dimension. We come as professional cyclists, and leave the rest of what we are at home. The only personal thing I take with me to bike races is a crucifix. I even leave my name. All my life I've been Victor

Hugo. That's what my parents called me, and that's the name my Colombian friends use. The only exception is my girlfriend Erica, who calls me, 'Mi amor'! In the team, most people call me 'Vic' or 'Tiburón,' my Spanish nickname. They don't translate it to 'Shark': it's 'Hey, Tiburón!' Lance sometimes calls me 'VH'; Johan calls me 'Victorrrr!' – he always exaggerates the 'r' – 'Victorrrr!' although if it's important, I'm either 'Peña!' or 'Victor!' I leave my clothes at home, too. When I was riding for Kelme and Vitalicio, we all wore the same team clothing, including the shoes. The Euskaltel-Euskadi riders all wear orange. The Kelmes and the ONCEs all have team wardrobes. At the airports, the iBanesto riders stand up when their team director stands up, and board the plane when he boards. US Postal is slightly more relaxed. The clothing is team clothing, but there's more variety. We have shirts in different colours. You can come down for dinner in shorts that don't belong to the team, or jeans that aren't team jeans.

When I first came to Europe, I saw people coloured their hair and wore earrings. But when I coloured my hair and had my ear pierced, my *directeur sportif* at Vitalicio, Javier Mínguez, told me, 'If you want to fix your hair like a queer, go and play soccer. Cycling is for men. You go through misery. You ride so hard you dribble, you shit yourself, you fall on your face and bleed, but you carry on. In cycling you earn your money going through hell. Why don't you learn to play football, where you kick the ball around for an hour a day and earn millions.' And it's true: at the end of a stage, you don't care what you look like. 'I survived' is all that matters. When I first came to Europe, there were moments in which I considered going back to Colombia to carry on cycling, but also to go to university and have the life that I didn't have as a kid because I was training instead of going out with my friends. Cycling closes your eyes and your social circle. You live in hotel rooms, like a clown in a mobile circus; and although you're always travelling, you never meet anyone, you can't visit anyone. It even takes your taste for travel away: when the season finishes, you don't want to go on holiday because you've been away all year. I remember that in 1996, I realised I didn't have any female friends. I didn't know a single woman! I'd lost contact with the girls I knew because I was always away. One day I said to myself, 'I'm alone. Cycling has made me alone.' I couldn't even eat an ice cream alone in the park because it's not part of my diet. I went to the cinema alone, and channelled the solitude into cycling. Every time I won a stage or a time trial, I thought, 'This is my reward.'

Still, I never considered giving up. In 1996 I had an accident two days before a national time trial championship. I'd just won the individual pursuit title, and I wanted to be like Chris Boardman and win the pursuit and the time trial, the first Colombian to win both national titles. But the fall put me out of the time trial, and when I saw my face in the mirror, I wept. I'd become a monster. It felt like an ordeal sent to test me, to ask, *Are you capable of going on?* I didn't think twice. I believe my life depends on my behaviour. I don't say one thing to someone's face, and another behind their back. I try to be organised, serious at work. If I'm good, then my results will be good.

I never lived that stage from eighteen to twenty-three when you're out partying, meeting girls, drinking. I'm only twenty-nine, but when I talk to a twenty-year-old I must sound like his father. I've never lived like a twenty-year-old. I've never thought like one. And although there are extrovert riders who say, 'In the winter I did this and that,' they did it for two months, not five years between the ages of eighteen and twenty-three. When I'm in Colombia, I go camping with friends, but I can't drink beer, or eat ice cream or chocolate. Cycling is a way of life. It changes your relationship with your girlfriend, for example. Her life is going to be very different from those of her friends. She won't be able to smoke. It's unlikely she'll have a Friday or Saturday night out during the season. In other sports, perhaps the best in each sport have this discipline, but not all of them. For the rest, sport allows them another life. Every single cyclist has this discipline, from Armstrong to the worst rider on the Tour. The difference is that Armstrong has two per cent more.

10

Luz-Ardiden

Monday 21 July 2003, 14:32: Col du Tourmalet

There must be forty left in the leading group, with a small line of riders just out of contact, five or six metres behind. All the riders in the top ten overall are present in the yellow jersey's pack. López de Munaín has already dropped out of the group. Chavanel is still nine minutes forty ahead. I'm second, over-heating as we pass spectators wrapped in overcoats against the mountain chill. Suddenly, Carlos Sastre, Francisco Mancebo and Christophe Moreau catapult upwards. I start to chase, but Iban Mayo sprints past. Triki follows and brings Mayo back, but Moreau persists. Ullrich, squat in the saddle like a power-lifter tensed for the weight, suddenly accelerates with incredible force; only Armstrong, leaning forward out of the saddle, can stay on his wheel. Moreau is caught and instantly dropped. Armstrong, sitting back in the saddle, sees a gap open behind the German. I can no longer match the accelerations of the climbers. My work is done, and I begin to lose ground. My moment of joy has ended.

When their job is done, some domestiques take their ear-piece out. Perhaps they do it to avoid the tension – emotional tension can drain you at the Tour. I keep mine in, listening, hoping. We all have a job to do and, up to the moment I finished mine and dropped off the front, everything has gone well. I'm sure Armstrong is going to finish the job, but in cycling, anything can happen, and I'm tense, listening to the emotion in Johan's voice, hoping to hear positive signs. He's encouraging Lance. It isn't a race commentary; it's more like listening to half a telephone conversation. Two days ago, on the stage to Bonascre, Johan was saying, 'That's it, Lance, carry on at your rhythm, go at your rhythm.' I thought Lance had attacked. Then I heard Johan say, 'Don't lose hope,' and I realised Jan was ahead. I thought Sastre was going to win the stage, with Lance second and Jan third. It turned out that Jan was second, gaining time on Lance, who was a couple of places behind. The signal comes and goes, but it gives you some idea of what's happening. Johan is saying to Lance, 'Let him go and keep him there.' He's passing on information, keeping the domestiques informed, and encouraging Lance: 'Triki, Chechu is twenty seconds behind you.'

As each minute grinds past, Ullrich's great limbs crank the heavy gear through eighty-five turns. The German enters a tunnel. Time elapses. Staring glassily into the immediate future, Armstrong enters, hummingbird-like: four seconds have passed. There is a confusion over scale. Four more seconds, and Mayo and Moreau enter the tunnel mouth. The absurdity of the intervals dazes you. Vinokourov, Zubeldia and Basso enter fifteen seconds behind Ullrich. In the frenzy of speed, Alexander Vinokourov struggles for breath behind the orange blur of Zubeldia.

The hours Iñigo Chaurreau has been alone dissipate in turbulence as Ullrich and, some time later, Armstrong shoot past. The speed disparity is bewildering. Still far from Ullrich's wheel, Armstrong rides out of the saddle. His wolf eyes glance behind. Mayo is thirty metres back. They return hungrily to their prey, that powerful stag ahead, perhaps too strong to be tackled. Ullrich veers across the road to keep his slipstream from the Texan. Armstrong homes in as if driven by some impersonal mechanism. At length, the German is caught. Mist makes the valley invisible. The dreamtime of his attack cannot be made commensurate with the four minutes, twenty-one seconds that have passed. Vinokourov is gasping to meet the payments his oxygen debt demands, insensible to Zubeldia and Basso at his elbows.

Mayo reaches Armstrong and Ullrich. A Portuguese flag is tortured frantically towards them by a man who sends punches into the air. Mayo attacks, out of the saddle. Armstrong immediately stands up in the pedals, but allows Ullrich to lead them both back to the Basque rider's wheel. Behind Mayo and Ullrich, Armstrong takes something from his pocket and eats, quietly storing fuel for the final climb. Half a minute back, Vinokourov's face speaks of shock: he is ten metres behind Ivan Basso. Tyler Hamilton and Georg Tötschnig, with Menchov and Sastre, reach Vinokourov. Hamilton pauses there for breath, then darts past. Vinokourov reacts, distances himself from Tötschnig, Menchov and Sastre, but cannot stay with Hamilton. Vinokourov stands up, sits low over the bars, stands up again, incoherent in his movements, the animation gone from his eyes.

Ullrich leads the trio. He accelerates. Then Mayo takes over, taking Armstrong with him. Haimar Zubeldia, the second Basque, flows forward without sound. He moves up behind the trio and slots into place. The Basque fans are in ecstasy. Further up the mountainside, Chavanel is among orange-shirted Basques who bait him with *irrukiñas* like toreadors before a bull. Blue sky appears through the haze. An uninterrupted file of riders – Dennis Menchov, Laurent Dufaux, Georg Tötschnig, Franco Pellizotti, Triki Beltrán, Jörg Jaksche, Aitor Garmendia, Chechu Rubiera, Roberto Laiseka, Patrice Halgand and Juan Miguel Mercado – reaches and begins to flow past Vinokourov. His face again crumples as Laiseka's wheel withdraws into the gradient ahead of him. Halgand dances past. Vinokourov is diminished, feeble in his pedal strokes, without vigour. He leans desperately forwards, as if by positioning his head four or five centimetres further forwards there will be less distance to pedal. An immense lurch into the pain brings him a breath closer to Halgand; seconds later, he drops back again.

Armstrong, Ullrich and the two Basques are consumed by sudden sunlight. They pass a sign reading 'Sommet 1 km.' Chavanel passed the same sign four minutes, twenty-eight seconds ago, entering a corridor of orange, yellow, red, blue, white and black, distributed before and around him on flags, banners, hats, T-shirts. A motorcycle fitted with crates of water bottles hovers off the chase. Armstrong signals and takes a *bidon*. He is able to think clearly, to plan ahead: rehydrate, refuel – success depends on it. The thick white rim of Ullrich's glasses accentuates the generosity of his phenotype. His plump face floats above the fatless torso, the chin unshaven like the hung-over clerk. Armstrong is angular, stretched skin over fleshlessness, cleanly shaven.

Chavanel's mouth, a nozzle at the end of a constricted breathing tube, half-grins to keep the passage open. Just behind him, Botero is almost stationary, standing on the pedals and waiting for his team-mate, now a minute behind the yellow-jersey group. Vinokourov gains Halgand's wheel again, and loses it again.

The crowd that four minutes ago healed behind Chavanel opens again and the yellow-jersey quartet scythes through lions of Flanders, the orange T-shirts of the Basques, and banners bearing CSC's corporate logo. Ullrich leads the foursome over the lip of the Col du Tourmalet and into the towering space of the abyss. One by one, the clock counts thirty-one seconds. Mcreau, Basso and Tyler Hamilton cross the col. Thirty-two more measured seconds. Tötschnig, Menchov, Sastre, Guerini, Beltrán, Rubiera, Jaksche, Laiseka and Garmendia pass.

Botero has found Vinokourov and pilots him towards the col. Each takes a bottle from the Team Telekom car. They cross the brow of the road one minute and eighteen seconds behind the yellow-jersey group. Vinokourov trails uselessly after him. Botero brakes to allow the Kazakh to reach his wheel, then sets off again.

Mayo, in an aerodynamic tuck, leads the four-man plummet. Behind him, Armstrong adjusts his shoes, earpiece, helmet strap; takes a bottle from his team car; chews solid food. Ullrich wobbles his thighs to loosen them and keep them warm. Botero and Vinokourov reach the back of the group containing Tötschnig, Menchov, Sastre, Guerini, Beltrán, Rubiera, Jaksche, Laiseka and Garmendia. Vino-kourov relents. Botero barks at him and leads him straight past the group. Rubiera catches their slipstream and the group follows at Botero's speed.

The race is stretched out over more than twenty kilometres. Simultaneously, Chavanel is beneath the 'Fifteen kilometres to the stage finish' banner at Luz-Saint-Saveur, bent into an aerodynamic teardrop with his torso below the collar-bones touching the handlebars and his face ten centimetres above his front wheel; Hamilton, Basso and Moreau catch

Armstrong, Ullrich, Mayo and Zubeldia; ten minutes and ten seconds behind them, Victor Hugo Peña reaches the brow of the Tourmalet climb with his team-mate Floyd Landis and a small group of stragglers, five minutes ahead of the final *gruppetto*.

Chavanel drinks, then rises out of the saddle and accelerates again. Ullrich takes a bottle, gel and two energy bars from his team car. Still led by Botero, the Vinokourov group passes under the 'Arrivée 20 km' banner as Chavanel turns on to the bridge over the Gave de Pau and on to the D12 that leads up to Luz-Ardiden. This is where the real climb begins. He drinks again. The yellow-jersey group crosses a zebra crossing on the descent into Luz-Saint-Saveur. Chavanel has gained time on them: Armstrong and Ullrich are waiting for their team-mates. Beltrán, Rubiera and Garmendia are in the Vinokourov group; they cannon over the zebra crossing less than a minute behind the yellow jersey.

On the slight incline before the bridge, Basso attacks. Mayo goes with him, before Ullrich leads Armstrong and the rest of the group back up to them. On the same ramp, Botero is jettisoned by the chase. His job is done. His team-mate Giuseppe Guerini now leads, his face contorted with pain. On the Tourmalet, the exchanges took place outside chronological time. At the foot of the final climb, every small discrepancy becomes significant. The yellow-jersey group of seven crosses on to the bridge five minutes and nine seconds after Chavanel passed this point. The pause to allow the Vinokourov group to reintegrate has allowed Chavanel to extend his lead by over a minute on the descent. On the first part of the climb, he gains a further fifteen seconds, and leads by five minutes and twenty-three seconds. The chasers are less than forty seconds behind the yellow-jersey group. Halgand is struggling to stay in contact. Then, less than two minutes after the group crossed the bridge, the red race car and motorcycles behind the yellow jersey move aside, allowing the two groups to merge. The two knots of riders unravel into one. The leading seven riders, and fifteen out of the top twenty riders in the general classification are as close now as they were at the stage start, over four hours ago. After two sprints, three fourth-category climbs, a first category and an *hors catégorie* climb, the same eighteen seconds separate the three GC leaders. Beltrán rides straight to the front; Garmendia passes him and raises the pace. Rubiera makes his way through the group. As they pass the village of Sazos, eleven and a half kilometres from the finish line, Garmendia leads Beltrán and Rubiera, followed by Ullrich, Armstrong and Vinokourov. Basso, Zubeldia, Mayo, Moreau and the rest of the group follow in their wake.

Victor Hugo is listening intently as the signal comes and goes:

When I hear Garmendia is leading the group and increasing the pace, I remember a climb called the Morredero during the Trofeo Castilla y León. It's 1998. I've just arrived in Europe after the Tour of Colombia. We begin the climb with the ONCE guys at the front, setting the pace. With ten kilometres to go there are only ten of us left in the group: Garmendia is beside me, Ullrich is there, too; so are two excellent Spaniards, Ángel Casero and Fernando Escartín, and another Colombian, Carlos Contreras. I don't see the others. It's too easy for me, too slow, so I attack. I'm fast, and only three of them can live with the pace: Garmendia, Casero and Escartín, three of the best climbers in the world. I work them over, we drop Casero, but in the last kilometre, Garmendia attacks. I don't have another acceleration in my legs and I can't stay with him, so I ride with Escartín. Garmendia wins the stage. I finish a few seconds later, with Escartín.

The following year, Escartín finished third in the Tour de France. My job now is to ride hard on the flat, and into the foothills, until I can't go on. I can feel my energy is going; my blood-sugar level is dropping. I have to keep drinking and eating.

The riders remove their helmets for the final climb. Hamilton hands his to the car of his former team, US Postal. Pellizotti, an Alessio rider, gives his to the ONCE-Eroski car. Beltrán takes over the chase from Garmendia. The pace is so high that a gap opens up behind Tötschnig: Jaksche is beginning to lose touch. Tötschnig is already adrift of Pellizotti, who is falling away from the leading group. Patrice Halgand sustains the pace for one minute longer, before surrendering to the pain of oxygen debt. Menchov resists for a further minute, then he too drops back.

It is four twenty-eight; 10.2 kilometres from the stage finish, the climb steepens. Mayo, still volatile, darts out of the group again. Armstrong straightens, extends his body forwards, angles his pedal stroke obliquely behind him and increases his leg speed and intensity in cruel acceleration. Unable to mimic such agility, Ullrich remains in the saddle and drives still more brute power into the pedals. Already much faster than Mayo and still accelerating, Armstrong flashes past him into a three-length lead, still bobbing over the saddle. Mayo somehow wrings more speed from his slight physique, inadvertently piloting the German into Armstrong's slipstream. Mayo sits; as he tries to find the oxygen that will take him into a region of less acute discomfort, Armstrong is still dancing over the saddle, rocking his bike from side to side, the colour fading from his face. A temporary stable state has been achieved. The trio is fifty seconds clear of the chasing group.

In twenty seconds, Armstrong spins the pedals forty times.

He brushes the spectators with his right arm, taking the shortest route around the right-hand curve. In the fluid continuum of motion, he rolls his bike to the right to compensate for the vertical and angled forces acting on his left pedal. A yellow blur appears beside his right hand, disk-like, tightening into a noose over the brake lever. A replica feedbag, flourished by a little boy in a green T-shirt and blue-peaked baseball hat. If he only opens his hand and surrenders his souvenir, the danger will pass. But the ephemera scattered from the caravan trigger a motor impulse, a muscular twitching in even the most detached personality: its boiled sweets and miniature cheeses have kindled his most infantile appetites. He has been standing for hours at this corner, hoping to see this phase dance between chaos and stability, but he scarcely even glimpses the riders as they pass, even on this steep stretch. To release his keepsake would be to lose the certainty that he has witnessed the Tour de France at all. It is unthinkable that he will loosen his grip. And so, of course, he holds it tight. The tension lasts perhaps a fifth of a second before the chord goes limp. Coordinates, moments, gyroscopic forces pass through complex equations, grids intersect, breaths of linear tension converge inwards, folding into tangents and arcs and, in an organised drift, Armstrong is suddenly released into free fall, man and bike twisting clockwise in the air, left shoulder lurching downwards, front wheel gliding away to the right, rear wheel rotating outwards. Armstrong extends an arm to break his fall and begin the roll that will disrupt the instantiated exchanges, deflecting the collision forces and bringing him to a halt on his back, facing the sky, legs extending down the slope. Before he reaches the road surface, Mayo runs into his rear wheel. His bike begins to drop away to the right. As Armstrong controls his fall, Mayo goes down to his left, breaks his fall with an outstretched arm and spins around, the automatic pedals not freeing his shoes until he is writhing on the asphalt. He comes to a halt sitting upright, looking back down the road beside Armstrong. It has taken perhaps half a second. Ullrich swerves around them both. Perhaps not knowing what to do, he checks his own bike for damage. Then he accelerates away.

In an instant, Mayo picks up his bike. A fan runs across the road and pushes Mayo, but too hard. He spins perpendicular to the road, panics, dismounts, remounts, before, this time, getting away, all so quickly that the chasing group, led by his team-mate Haimar Zubeldia, has still not reached him. Armstrong takes longer: his chain is jammed. He finally pulls away ten seconds after Mayo, twenty-five seconds after the fall. Just ahead of him he finds Rubiera, who lowers his hand in a gesture meaning, *It's OK, calm yourself*. They speed past Sastre and spy the orange jerseys of Roberto Laiseka and Iban Mayo. Jan Ullrich, Ivan Basso, Haimar Zubeldia, Christophe Moreau, Tyler Hamilton and Alexander Vinokourov are forty metres further up the incline. The chasing group is stretched out along seventy metres of the climb. If Ullrich has waited, it is at such speed that Vinokourov is having to stand up on the pedals to maintain the waiting pace.

Mayo hugs the left-hand side of the road. Overtaking him, Armstrong enters that phase in the liquid dance that propels him onwards in which the bike inclines to the left as the opposite pedal descends and rotates. Under the pressure of his bodyweight, his right foot slips out of the pedal. The bike tilts so far to the left that his left foot is forced out of its pedal. In one movement, the rear wheel loses adhesion and skids out to the left and into the road, and his torso descends until his sternum strikes the handlebars. Mayo darts around him.

Armstrong has lost both his momentum and his team-mate's wheel. He painstakingly inserts the cleat of his shoe into the pedal. He cannot change gears, and labours before he can get up to speed, staring down at his feet in disbelief.

Four-thirty. With nine and a half kilometres of climbing to the stage finish, Ivan Basso raises his glasses on to his forehead and slows. Ullrich looks over his right shoulder, and seeing little, rides over to the right-hand side of the road for a better view. Hamilton moves to the front and gestures with his right hand, 'Wait.' Ten seconds later, on Rubiera's wheel, Armstrong reaches the group. They pass Vinokourov, Zubeldia, Hamilton, Basso and Moreau. Ullrich looks several times over his right shoulder at the yellow jersey in a show of concern. The group coheres for a few seconds before Mayo attacks yet again. Ullrich leads the chase back up to Mayo, who drops back into the bunch. Rubiera moves to the front of the group with Armstrong just behind.

Two minutes pass. Then Mayo goes again. Armstrong rides around Rubiera and accelerates. Once again, in an almost exact repetition of events that took place no more than four minutes ago yet, in the anxious logic that shapes the race, belong to a now inaccessible past, Armstrong catches Mayo in an instant and rides straight past at great speed. As Mayo, once again, pushes himself into oxygen depletion to make it into Armstrong's slipstream, Ullrich's immense power begins to lift him away from the group until, just as abruptly, he desists, as if a sudden spark of fear or recognition has activated some inner tripping mechanism. Instead of entering the solitary chase, he looks over his shoulder at Basso, then, in order, Zubeldia, Hamilton, Moreau. He eases the downward force, and the five suddenly form a single, connected file. Meanwhile, Mayo drops off Armstrong's pace, and both men find themselves alone, one leading, the other unable to stay on his wheel.

There is a dark blemish on Armstrong's yellow jersey, over his left shoulder blade, where he fell. His eyebrows are raised, ruffling his forehead: he stares down the doubt that he may be destined to lose this race, the supervising consciousness insisting that he will not be able to maintain this degree of discomfort. His mouth is open, as if he has just finished holding his breath underwater, and has surfaced, gasping for air. Sweat drips from his chin.

Ullrich clutches vainly at the brittle figment ahead of him. His efforts are no less extreme. Great creases have formed over his eyes, and swollen pouches under them. His cheeks have darkened. His jaw is gaping and his shoulders are arched in pain, as if struggling against some irresistible gravity that distorts his features and threatens to engulf him. The four riders on his wheel – Basso, Zubeldia, Moreau, Hamilton – are gasping for breath. Unable to stay with them, Vinokourov has dropped back, with Rubiera following him.

Four forty-four. Armstrong rounds a right-hand bend to see Sylvain Chavanel ahead of him. Still seated, he rides up in Chavanel's slipstream, pulls out to the right, and without slowing down or breaking his concentration, gives the French-man a pat on the small of the back. A few metres ahead of Chavanel, he rises out of the saddle and accelerates again. Chavanel has a severe, fleshless face, pursed lips, and is rolling from side to side.

Victor Hugo is approaching the point where his leader fell, twenty-five minutes ago:

An ONCE team car comes alongside. I ask the car driver for water to wash down a high energy-bar. He gives me a *bidon*. I ask him,

'How are they going?' He says, 'Your boss is alone.' It's then I see the fall on the tiny TV screen mounted on the console. This can't be happening. Why is it that everything happens to Lance? I think it's live, five kilometres from the stage finish. No, this is a recording. He fell at the bottom of the climb. He shows me where the fall had taken place. But where's Lance? Out on his own. And I think, *This guy's amazing*. I go back to the group, and tell Floyd and Eki, *Lance is alone, but he fell at the bottom*. We all ride close to spectators. We try to take the shortest distance, and that's where the public is. I've hit spectators with my shoulders. You try to cover the handlebars. When we're leading him, Lance sometimes says, 'Not so close to the people.' In the space of ten seconds, I realise he's fallen, remounted and carried on, and now has a twenty-five-second lead. I began to hear Johan on the radio, motivating him: 'Forty seconds. That's you, Armstrong.' I don't need to see television pictures. I've spent hours and hours behind Lance, watching him dance out of the saddle with an incredible cadence. At last, Armstrong is riding like Armstrong. I know how he is. At moments like these, he wants to devour the world.

At war with their bodies, Armstrong and Ullrich punish themselves to conjure up more speed. Armstrong passes the 'Arrivée 4 km' sign forty-eight seconds ahead of Ullrich. Over the next kilometre, Ullrich gains eight seconds. His pace begins to suffocate Christophe Moreau, who drops behind. Even so, Armstrong pulls back eleven seconds over the following kilometre.

At four fifty-three and thirty-seven seconds, Armstrong passes beneath the red kite that marks one kilometre to go. His head is gradually lowering, his eyes sinking into their sockets beneath his folding brow. Less and less of the road ahead falls within his diminishing field of vision. Still he rises out of the saddle and increases the power and the pain. Sweat drips from the point of his nose.

Jan Ullrich passes beneath the red kite forty-eight seconds behind Armstrong: he has regained three seconds. It takes Armstrong twelve seconds to cross from the '500 m to go' banner to the '400 m to go' sign, and a further twelve seconds to reach the '300 m to go' sign. Fifty-six seconds later he crosses the finish line at Luz-Ardiden. He throws his bike forward like a sprinter desperate to gain a few extra centimetres. His eyes, sunken into the skull, have become small and crossed; deep furrows have appeared over his cheekbones, beneath the eye sockets. The skin of his face is taut and pale; the lines around his nose and mouth have become deep, as if the centre of his face were contracting in pain. Beneath their bones, his cheeks are cratered into tortured crescents. His journey into pain and self-diminishment has taken four hours, twenty-nine minutes and twenty-six seconds. Ullrich claws back eight seconds over the final kilometre, although Mayo steals second place and four time-bonus seconds. Vinokourov arrives two minutes and forty seconds after Armstrong. Armstrong has gained fifty-two seconds on Ullrich – less than 300 metres. Vinokourov comes in two minutes, seven seconds behind. A rout in a 5000-metre run: a heartbeat after 149.5 kilometres.

Luz-Ardiden. After the stage, Lance got on the team bus. It was the most euphoric day for Lance since I've known him. I've seen him happy before, but never like this. He stormed up and down the aisle, punching the seats and shouting, 'No one trains like me. No one rides like me. This jersey's mine. I live for this jersey. It's my life. No one's taking it away from me while I'm around. This fucking jersey's mine.' *After all those hours of effort, planning, training*, he was saying, *I'm the one that does this best*. He was shouting for himself, shouting for the rest of us, shouting with excitement, happiness, fear and anger. Fear, because Lance usually has everything under control: now he was showing that something he dearly wanted had nearly slipped out of reach. Anger, because when he heard Rudy Pevenage thought Ullrich would soon have the yellow jersey, he was enraged. He took that anger out on the final climb. As I looked at him, I thought, *Look what meaning that jersey has. Look how much it means.*

Finally, we saw Armstrong's eyes. At dinner, we saw the real Armstrong again. He said to the masseurs, 'Come and sit with us.' Armstrong style. He told us he'd been ashamed of looking at us, he'd felt he was failing us: we were working hard and he'd been failing us.

Stage 15: Bagnères-de-Bigorre–Luz-Ardiden
Distance: 159.5 km
Winner's time: 4 hrs 29 mins 26 secs
Winner's average speed: 35.519 kph
Starters: 154, Finishers: 151

	1 (20 sec bonus)	Lance ARMSTRONG (USP/USA)
40 secs	2 (12 sec bonus)	Iban MAYO (EUS/ESP)
same time	3 (8 sec bonus)	Jan ULRICH (TBI/GER)
same time	4	Zubeldia (EUS/ESP)
43 secs	5	C. Moreau (CA/FRA)
47 secs	6	Basso (FAS/ITA)
1 min 10	7	Hamilton (CSC/USA)
2 mins 07	8	Vinokourov (TEL/KAZ)
2 mins 45	9	Rubiera (USP/ESP)
2 mins 47	10	Chavanel (BLB/FRA)
3 mins 12	11–13	Sastre (CSC/ESP), Menchov (BAN/RUS), Laiseka (EUS/SPA)
3 mins 24	14–15	Totschnig (GST/AUT), Beltrán (USP/ESP)
4 mins 10	16	Jaksche (ONE/GER)
4 mins 25	17	Pellizotti (ALS/ITA)
5 mins 27	18	Halgand (DEL/FRA)
5 mins 36	19–20	Mancebo (BAN/ESP), Luttenberger (CSC/AUT)
6 mins 17	21	Boogerd (RAB/HOL)
7 mins	22	Rous (BLB/FRA)

....

' mins 21	23	Azevedo (ONE/POR)
mins 03	24	Gutierrez (KEM/ESP)
mins 49	25–27	Goubert (DEL/FRA), Virenque (QSD/FRA), Mercado (BAN/ESP)
mins 15	28–29	Plaza (TBI/ESP), Garcia Casas (TBI/ESP)
mins 49	30	Guerini (TEL/ITA)
0 mins 13	31–33	Astarloza (A2R/ESP), Chaurreau (A2R/ESP), Van de Wouwer (QSD/BEL)
0 mins 40	34	Lelli (COF/ITA)
1 mins 4	35	Brochard (A2R/FRA)
1 mins 11	36–37	Bruseghin (FAS/ITA), N. Sorensen (CSC/DAN)
1 mins 16	38	Dufaux (ALS/SUI)
1 mins 53	39	Fritsch (FDJ/FRA)
2 mins 26	40	Ludewig (SAE/GER)
2 mins 56	41	Garmendia (TBI/ESP)
3 mins 37	42	Blaudzun (CSC/DAN)
6 mins 26	43–50	Freire (RAB/ESP), Casero (TBI/ESP), Pascual Llorente (KEM/ESP), Portal (A2R/FRA), Rogers (QSD/AUS), Botcharov (A2R/RUS), Flickinger (A2R/FRA), Kessler (TEL/GER)
17 mins 40	51	Niermann (RAB/GER)
19 mins 49	52–56	Hincapie (USP/USA), O'Grady (CA/AUS), Botero (TEL/COL), Pineau (BLB/FRA), Zandio (BAN/ESP)
23 mins 02	57–72	Cañada (QSD/ESP), Brandt (LOT/BEL), Beneteau (BLB/FRA), Miholjevic (ALS/CRO), Lopez de Munaín

....

(EUS/ESP), Nozal (ONE/ESP), Bolts (GST/GER), Bodrogi (QSD/HUN), Lastras (BAN/ESP), Nardello (TEL/ITA), Aerts (TEL/BEL), Zampieri (CAL/SUI), Latasa (KEM/ESP), Artetxe (EUS/ESP), Vasseur (COF/FRA), Andrle (ONE/CZE)

23 mins 21	73	Cioni (FAS/ITA)
25 mins 7	74–75	Bettini (QSD/ITA), Paolini (QSD/ITA)
25 mins 28	76	Commesso (SAE/ITA)
28 mins 36	77–97	Sacchi (SAE/ITA), Peron (CSC/ITA), Noè (ALS/ITA), Landis (USP/USA), Geslin (BLB/FRA), Pradera (ONE/ESP), Zabel (TEL/GER), Serrano (ONE/ESP), Ekimov (USP/RUS), Hary (BLB/FRA), Aldag (TEL/GER), Karpets (BAN/RUS), Landaluze (EUS/ESP), Cuesta (A2R/ESP), Piil (CSC/DAN), N. Jalabert (CSC/FRA), Peña (USP/COL), Peschel (GST/GER), Lefèvre (DEL/FRA), Baguet (LOT/BEL), Renier (BLB/FRA)
34 mins 44	98–149	Liese (TBI/GER), Flecha (BAN/ESP), Knaven (QSD/HOL), Van Bon (LOT/HOL), García Acosta (BAN/ESP), Becke (TBI/GER), D. Muñoz (KEM/ESP), De Groot (RAB/HOL), Clain (COF/FRA), Christensen (CSC/DAN), Millar (COF/GBR), Gonzalez de Galdeano (ONE/ESP), Hinault (CA/FRA), Gaumont (COF/FRA), Edaleine (DEL/FRA), Bossoni (CAL/ITA), Guidi (TBI/ITA), Usano (KEM/ESP), McGee (FDJ/AUS), Cooke (FDJ/AUS), Padrnos (USP/CZE), Dumoulin (DEL/FRA), Heras (USP/ESP), Krivtsov (DEL/UKR), M. Zberg (GST/SUI), Poilvet (CA/FRA), Casar (FDJ/FRA), Simoni (SAE/ITA), Fornaciari (SAE/ITA), Mengin (FDJ/FRA), Moncoutié (COF/FRA), Glomser (SAE/AUT), Hushovd (CA/NOR), Andriotto (CAL/ITA), Wielinga (RAB/HOL), Trentin (COF/ITA), Wauters (RAB/BEL), Vogondy (FDJ/FRA), Parra (KEM/COL), Oriol (A2R/FRA), Bramati (QSD/ITA), Turpin (A2R/FRA), Da Cruz (FDJ/FRA), J. P. Nazon (DEL/FRA), McEwen (LOT/AUS), Petrov (BAN/RUS), Voeckler (BLB/FRA),

		Gates (LOT/AUS), Vainsteins (CAL/LAT), Finot (DEL/FRA), D. Nazon (BLB/FRA), Moerenhout (LOT/HOL)
34 mins 54	150	Bertolini (ALS/ITA)
35 mins 35	151	De Clercq (LOT/BEL)

Did not start: Milesi (CAL/ITA)
Abandons: Bertagnolli (ISAE/ITA), F. Rodriguez (CAL/USA)
Outside time limit: Merckx (LOT/BEL)

The Weightless, Invisible Sport

The boulevard that starts at the Arc de Triomphe as Avenue de Friedland and ends at the Place de la République as Boulevard St-Martin passes through seven identities and five *arrondissements* on its four-kilometre meander through the heart of Paris. Between the segments known as Boulevard Haussmann and Boulevard Poissonnière, not far from the Opéra and within walking distance of the Palais Royale, one block assumes the alias Boulevard Montmartre – prime city real estate, every square inch of which is made to yield a profit and always has. The most opulent of the nineteenth-century arcades that tunnel perpendicularly away from the street is the Galerie Vivienne, first enlarged to create more boutique space as long ago as 1831. The designer-clothing franchises and jewellers that line the pavement are part of a long tradition.

Camille Pissarro, who painted it in 1897 from a hotel room on the corner of the Boulevard des Italiens and the Rue Drouot, would recognise much of the scene today: the Théâtre des Variétés; the Hôtel Ronceray, now part of a global chain. What he would make of the Hard Rock Café, we can't say, but he would certainly miss the Café de Madrid. The Madrid had already been a favourite haunt for journalists, critics and writers for four decades as Pissarro charged his brush. Five years later, on 20 November 1902, when the normally unapproachable Henri Desgrange, director of *L'Auto*, surprised his chief cycling correspondent Géo Lefèvre by inviting him to lunch, the Madrid remained the natural choice. Minutes earlier, in *L'Auto*'s offices around the corner at 10 Rue du Faubourg-Montmartre, Desgrange had asked his staff for suggestions that could boost circulation and safeguard their jobs. Lefèvre's contribution was, *What about a bicycle race around France in several stages, with rest days*? The two men elaborated on the idea over lunch: the Tour de France was not conceived at the Café de Madrid, but it received its first examination there.

I wandered the Boulevard in the brilliant June sunshine, just weeks before the start of the Centenary Tour, sniffing out some memory of its origins a hundred years before. The sign above a doorway on the south side read '—drid': I wondered if this was the place. The door was ajar, and I stepped inside. The seat backs of flexed cane tangled in heaps of ancient furniture made me think of Charlie Chaplin. Someone – the owner, perhaps – appeared from the back, only to disappoint me. He came to the door and gestured: *that* was where the old Madrid had stood. My heart sank as I crossed the street. The burger bar named Sunset Boulevard wasn't yet open for lunch. The waiter and waitress, one American, the other British, kindly let me walk around, despite the fact that neither knew of any commemorative plaque, or was even quite sure what I meant by the Tour de France. The walls were lined with sports memorabilia – baseball bats, shirts, cigarette cards – much of it either authentic or finished with a convincing aged-look glaze. Considerable efforts had clearly been made to wipe away all traces of history and replace them with a fantasy past – a futile dissimulation for an unreality that paled beside the truth.

I almost missed the old pig-iron bike – as far from a racing bike, even an early racing bike, as could be imagined – that hung from the ceiling, in front of a photograph of Maurice Garin, apparently cut from a magazine, and a 'Café de Madrid' menu in a frame, albeit one recent enough to have an eight-figure Parisian telephone number embossed at the foot of the front page. And such pains had been taken over every other exhibit! I showed the formal courtesies and left, irritated with the Sunset Boulevard for being such an unthinking product of its time but also with myself. What had I expected? A shrine? Desgrange and Lefèvre themselves, deep in conversation over a lobster? There's no *primum*, no historical source that really is the source, the font of unmediated truth. That I knew. But there are more deep-seated feelings than mere knowledge.

Yet disappointment felt the appropriate emotion for this awkward, in-between sport. For even if the print media adopted cycling early in their history, and in many cases have grown in symbiosis with the sport, the journalist whose task it is to recreate a race has as little access to the unmediated truth as I had in that bogus burger bar. He cannot merely piece together scattered shards to reassemble a vase, or gradually open the shutters until the view is totally clear. Nothing is more mediated than a totality. Yes, he compiles the most accurate architecture possible: was the attack before or after the village? Who made the first move? Who threw themselves body and soul into the breakaway, and who was hitching a cheap ride? And of course, he speaks to as many of those close to the action as he can, which means mastering many languages and charming riders keen to talk to their national media or facing a long drive to the hotel, before they can shower, take a massage, have dinner and make a hurried phone call home. This unsatisfactory rush leaves him with parts of wholes, broken pieces of narrative that refuse to sit together and require the insertion of connecting clauses, in a sport in which the connecting clauses *are* the narrative, so that the task of reconstruction resembles the philological work of assembling contradictory fragments of ancient myths, using far-flung sources that refuse to yield a simple and consistent story. Worse, he has to attribute intentions – to enter the athlete's mind and reconstruct what he imagines it sees. Yet every rider reads the race differently. How many commentators accurately read Jakob Piil's mind when his breakaway companion Fabio Sacchi offered him his hand as they entered the long final straight at Marseille? What did Piil understand from Sacchi's gesture? Was it, *I surrender*? Or, *If you want to come second, follow me*? Or simply, *Thanks for the company*? After the stage, Piil told me the answer: 'I don't understand a word of Italian,' he said. 'I have no idea what he was trying to say.'

The journalist, then, has to interpret his heap of incomplete information as personally as the conductor of an orchestra interprets a score, or the psychoanalyst a dream. Meanings echo off into infinity, history recedes from killing accelerations and abrupt crises into feigned attacks, darting looks, momentary anxieties, muscular tensions, fields of nerve impulses, polarity changes within the neuron membrane, vibrations passed over elementary distances. An impossible history of signals that elude recollection, resist language, evade any form of expression but the race itself. The whole endeavour of reconstructing cycling races as printed narratives, then, looks strangely like so many phony pieces of memorabilia in a badly lit bar, and leaves the public with summaries that are often partial, sometimes disproportionate, and enlivened by writers who at best see things incompletely. The earliest cycling journalists gleaned their fleeting perceptions of the race by pedalling alongside the riders to interview them, before dropping back, boarding the next train, and rejoining them later in the stage. Covering the first Tour for the journal *Le Vélo*, Robert Coquelle was reputed to be able to stay with the *routiers* for many kilometres, allowing him to collect exclusive insights – or so his newspaper boasted. With these beginnings, we might expect every newspaper account, every cycling book, to crackle with incompatible detail.

That they don't is largely due to those relative newcomers, radio and television broadcasting. The first Tour de France radio reports were made in 1929, and intensified the following year. Since 1958, an internal radio service, Radio Tour, has been relaying information and instructions from the race director's car behind the leading group of riders to the following vehicles, including team cars and journalists. By logging the communications of Radio Tour, journalists can compile an authoritative chronology of the unfolding of the stage, as seen from the race director's vehicle.

Until 1948, moving pictures of the Tour were restricted to cinema news packages. That year, the start of the Tour was first shown live. In 1967, slow-motion replays and displays allowing information to be superimposed on the screen became possible, allowing tabulated information previously only available in the press to be shown. In 1972, live colour images of the Tour were broadcast for the first time, and a system of motorbike cameras and helicopter relays pioneered: it is still largely in place. By 1976, even the great climbs could be broadcast live. Television has removed the journalists from the roads and confined them to the press room, where they follow the images on monitors. By switching between cameras trained at each group, television allows more of the race than ever to enter the visible realm. By doing so, a self-evidently fragmented experience of the race is replaced with representations that pass through the filter of the controlling producer before providing the press room and the television audience with an illusion of total access. This illusion has made cycling accessible to a mass global public: to be left breathless by the sight of tiny clusters of colour on the slopes of a vast Pyrenean massif as knots of tortured riders sift rare nuggets of oxygen from the gathering altitude, no prior knowledge is required. Yet compare cycling with boxing: where one allows its protagonists to emerge over hours from a huge darting shoal, the other features two readily identifiable athletes competing in short, literally punchy rounds punctuated by regular pauses; where the drama of one lies in a sudden acceleration after a preamble that can last all day, the other is a flashing display of deft blows and feints. No wonder boxing's Hollywood portrayal has been so distinguished, and cycling's so poor: the literalism of the moving image overlooks cycling's play of mystery and revelation. The printed word and the radio report can focus on the essence of the race: its overall structure, and the extraordinary work rate of hearts and lungs – both of which evade the cameras. In the years before television, fans probed the great cycling races with their imagination; today, we are invited to scan their surface with no more than our eyes.

These innovations, together with the post-stage press conference, which evolved from arrangements made to protect Eddy Merckx – forced by constant media demands to limit his press contact to a scheduled daily meeting – have standardised the narratives of the Tour. If it isn't communicated via Radio Tour, seen on television or mentioned at the press conference, it hasn't happened. And if it has been, it happened the way they describe it. Not knowing, which we cannot bear, is replaced by certainty. Sport becomes a finite, authorised canon of facts and anecdotes, measured, recorded and regurgitated in endless identical newspaper reports and an entire genre of cut-and-paste history books; and in this publishing frenzy, the domestique and his unseen stream of air, a physical gift paid for with pain that wipes the mind clean and constricts the vision, remain strangely absent. An entire history is suppressed. The domestique reminds us that we should never again tell a story as if it were the only story.

Yet it is not print journalism but television that has brought cycling to a new audience in recent years, aided by images and narratives that have caught the imagination of the global public: Chris Boardman's first futuristic time-trial bike; Miguel Induráin's remarkable heart, with its resting pulse of twenty-eight beats per minute; and those miracle tales – Greg Lemond's recovery from a hunting accident in April 1987 that left him minutes from bleeding to death to win two Tours de France, and Lance Armstrong's triumph over cancer, the bogeyman illness of the wealthy world, and the remarkable athletic achievements that followed.

If the first road racers exemplified the values of the early industrial bourgeoisie, their modern counterparts are startling embodiments of the business philosophy, developed in the mid-1980s, that successful corporations should primarily produce brands as opposed to products. The goods to which these brands attach, and by extension all industrial production of goods with any physical weight, began to be disparaged as 'lumpy objects'. Corporations that had until recently been weighed down with factories housing full-time, permanent workforces, and all the responsibilities they implied, could now be described as attempting to free themselves from the corporeal world of commodities. Manufacturing was farmed out to contractors, sometimes in very low-wage free-trade zones in poor nations, freeing management to elaborate corporate mythologies, viewing themselves less as providers of goods and services than as managers of weightless, intellectual capital including design, image development and brand extensions. Sport is heavily implicated in this sometimes extremely exploitative transformation. Phil Knight, the creator of Nike, one of Lance Armstrong's key corporate endorsers, has said, 'There is no market in making things any more. The value is added by careful research, by innovation and by marketing.' Like these great corporations, the riders and their equipment are tending towards weightlessness. Every ounce of excess flesh is stripped from the riders' bones; the equipment is pared down to the bare essentials. The bicycle is an elemental design. Considerable research goes into selecting materials with the optimal weight-to-strength ratio for their tasks, from expensive metals to carbon and ceramic composites. Contemporary frame technology borrows its materials from Formula One (high modulus carbon) and the aerospace industry (aluminium alloys, titanium and, most recently, magnesium). It uses computer-assisted design, stress analysis, and metal-working tools from the automobile sector (CNC machining). Firms now specialise in individual materials (carbon fibre, titanium, aluminium) and produce individual components (seat posts, headsets, wheels). Every part is subjected to exhaustive virtual and real stress and deformation testing. Wind-tunnel testing is an integral part of product development. Every square millimetre is designed. And like Schwarzenegger, the bicycle industry revels in military associations. The wheels used by Jan Ullrich are reportedly manufactured by former military engineers using carbon-working techniques unknown in the civil sector. The manufacturer of the bikes used by the US Postal riders boasts that the compressed carbon fibre/epoxy composite employed in their frames is 'designed to withstand the same stress forces as an F-16 fighter at Mach-2'. The finish of carbon stays, seat tubes and time-trial bars is in the sinister grey of the stealth bomber; the pixillated weave of the carbon mimics the on-screen drafts of computer design graphics, gesturing towards the weightlessness of pure information.

Fulvio Acquati, managing director of Deda Elementi, the prestigious Italian brand that produces Lance Armstrong's handlebars, insists on the weightlessness of his company's assets:

Deda Elementi's essential competence lies in project management. Our basic capital is design expertise, and a long tradition in racing. Where our designs are translated into solid objects is unimportant, so our products are manufactured wherever it is strategically advantageous to produce them. Design is everything. We have to provide our shareholders with a return on their investment, which means our products have to be successful in the marketplace, but that in turn means that they have to be successful on the Izoard and the Tourmalet, because we have to provide our customers with excellent products.

The manufacture of the modern, lightweight racing bike and its individual components is beginning to reflect the weightless logic. With the passing of the age of heavy industry in the West, a huge proportion of the world's bicycles designed there are manufactured in high-tech factories in Taiwan, where CNC technology and expertise in carbon working is combined with low wages. Yet only one manufacturer present at the Tour, Giant, is officially a Taiwanese firm. The weightless economy depends on a rigid separation of roles, at the base of which is a vast and anonymous workforce. When the history of cycling brought the domestique into being, it was a merely technical solution before the facts of fluid mechanics. As the domestiques drop away after pouring their energy into the air on the way to the race's glorious conclusion, cycling seems to tell of the emergence of hierarchy and anonymous travail. The domestique's suppression in writing and reflection about cycling seems to confirm the hypothesis. The medal table of the Olympic Games and every major world championships, the results sheet from the FIFA World Cup Finals and the General Classification of the Tour de France all give a relentlessly hierarchical picture of the modern community of nations.

Yet the bicycle itself is a perplexing icon. In an age of almost ubiquitous micro-computers, it brings with it nostalgia for the dying skills of the traditional craftsman. Artisans such as Edoardo Bianchi, Ernesto Colnago, Ugo De Rosa, the Pinarello brothers, Alfredo Gios and Dario Pegoretti began as framebuilders working by hand. Beside their hand-built output, all but Pegoretti now outsource their frames – gaining in productivity, losing in authenticity. And, at a time of rich-world over-consumption and sedentary obesity, the bicycle's fusion of machine and muscle power is a backward-looking mix. The self-sacrifice structured into the physics of cycling is at odds with the instant pleasures of consumer culture. The harsh desire to endure it embodies contrasts markedly with a mass culture predicated on the short concentration span. And for humanity's impoverished majority, the bicycle serves as a constant reminder of underdevelopment. If progress has come to mean primarily automation, increased material comfort and reduced physical labour, cycling at the start of the twenty-first century fosters doubts about the trajectory of the present, characterised by Western brains directing Third World brawn. Like other globalised industries, bicycle manufacture increasingly relies on cheap labour in places like Taiwan to realise designs created in the wealthy West – a system not unlike the division of labour between leaders and domestiques.

It's a logic that is repeated in every field that touches professional cycling. As time passes, the number of nationalities and identities represented among the riders increases, but the decision-making cadres – sponsors, *directeurs sportifs*, technical and support staff – continue to represent a few wealthy nations. Technicians from the periphery have no means of entry. The developing world is invited to host races and to send its most talented athletes to enrich the profession in the West, but when they return home to countries with sometimes weak states, poor police forces and endemic poverty, they find the wages of global sport create both insecurity and a sense of dislocation. Generations of athletes are driven abroad, and the young in the developing world are given a model of emigration by local heroes who become standard-bearers for rich-world paymasters. That the model is relevant to only an infinitesimally small and prodigiously gifted minority merely makes it more pernicious. Teams from beyond Western Europe and the Anglo-Saxon world are not welcome at major global cycling events, yet there are few world-rankings points to be won by remaining at home. The only major cycling event still disputed between national teams is the World Championships. Yet few among the general public know who the world champion is: the championships are peripheral, especially in their current calendar slot. What a contrast with soccer, in which the FIFA World Cup is the most prestigious tournament, and victory regularly goes to a developing nation. In cycling, the brain–brawn division is as deep as ever, and institutionally entrenched. Decision-making is power; the developing world is denied any. The committees of cycling's world governing body are chaired by West Europeans.

This closed form of globalisation is a paradoxical fate for a sport with such an open range of meanings. Shortly after hostilities ceased in post-Taliban Afghanistan, the first bike race was held on the road north from Kabul to Charikar. What better way of showing that the roads and bridges were intact and the snipers and mines had been cleared? In 2003, the international cycling calendar opened with the Tour of the Táchira in Venezuela, where supporters of President Chávez beat pots and pans to cheer on the cyclists, while his opponents whistled. Its geographical dimension allows cycling to be a topical means of national expression: certainly, the cultures where cycling is most deeply engrained today – including Belgium, the Basque Country, Brittany, Colombia and the regions of northern Italy – are places of strong local identity, burdened with the sense that their integrity and identity are endangered by anything from national absorption in the case of the regions, internal linguistic and religious divisions in the case of Belgium, an albeit increasingly distant past of cruel linguistic and cultural oppression in the Basque Country and, in Colombia, longstanding civil violence. If cycling races yield an emotional return that exceeds the local inconvenience they cause, it is surely because these populations gain some veiled psychic fulfilment from the completion, in emotional scenes of triumph, of arduous athletic odysseys across their land. By drawing symbolic lines between disparate locations, they translate the perceived threat of territorial defilement into celebrations of local identity that attract great public enthusiasm. Where no such threat is perceived, as in the Anglo-Saxon nations, we must suspect that, however successful national cyclists become, cycling will fail to mobilise the imaginary capital to become more than a minority sport.

Brands use athletes much as kings, bishops, nobles and patricians once treated artists: as servants of their power, with the consequence that Victor Hugo Peña's Colombia, to take one example, is awash with merchandise – genuine and counterfeit – bearing the brands endorsed by its greatest sportsmen: Compaq and BMW (Juan Pablo Montoya), Deutsche Telekom and T-Mobile (Santiago Botero), and, of course, the US Postal Service and Berry Floors. If Armstrong is the descendant of the Renaissance artist, his domestiques are the studio assistants who grind the paint, prime the panels, copy their master's cartoon and complete the peripheral detail before he brings his spark of genius. The traditional artist's apprenticeship has been to copy the work of the masters; in cycling, the masters do not want their virtuosity challenged, let alone excelled. As Lance Armstrong says, 'The Tour isn't about having nine guys who can win, it's about having one guy who can win and eight guys who can help him win.' So with his own opportunities for self-expression restricted to one or two early- or late-season events, the domestique's condition resembles a Faustian pact gone wrong – granted immense gifts, he is constrained to apply them only for another's glory. If sport bears some of the fire of artistic inspiration, the domestique reminds us of what must be discarded in creation: the chippings left by Michelangelo, the endless excisions made by Proust.

As we have seen, the route map of the first Tour de France gave the French a rare image of their country's geography at the turn of the twentieth century. Sport performs an analogous function in the wider world today. Cities compete to host major sporting events partly in order to enter the mental atlas of the global audience. Nonetheless, the easy identity between athlete and nation propagated in those orderly charts is false. The sprinter Jan Svorada competed as a Slovakian in 1993 before winning stage seven of the 1994 Tour as a representative of the Czech Republic. Lucien Petit-Breton (France), the first rider to win two Tours de France (at least, the first to do so legally: 1903 champion Maurice Garin won the 1904 Tour before he was retrospectively disqualified), had been born in Buenos Aires and had spent much of his youth there. The winner of stage eleven of the 2003 Tour, Juan Antonio Flecha (Spain), was also born in Buenos Aires, yet no 'official' Argentine has ever ridden the Tour. Two official Venezuelans have participated. The first, Leonardo Sierra, was born in Colombia before, still a child, crossing the Venezuelan border illegally with his parents. Only when Sierra was called up to the national team did the Venezuelan authorities notice his statelessness and issue the necessary documents. More recently, Unai Etxebarria of Euskaltel-Euskadi, the Basque national team, was born in Venezuela but has spent most of his life in the Basque Country and considers himself of Basque nationality. For this reason, Etxebarria has not sought a Spanish passport. He rides for Venezuela by default.

More complex predicaments have faced riders from the former Soviet Union. Djamoladine Abdoujaparov represented the Soviet Union in 1990 and 1991, before competing as an Uzbek between 1992 and 1997. The first Latvian to win stages and achieve a top-three finish, Piotr Ugrumov, is the son of a Russian father and Lithuanian mother who met and still reside in Riga. Ugrumov held Soviet papers until 1992, before becoming one of Latvia's 600,000 officially stateless residents, mostly of Russian, Belorussian and Polish origins. In 1995, after he had finished second in the 1993 Giro d'Italia, second in the 1994 Tour de France and third in the 1995 Giro, he was finally offered Latvian papers. Not so his parents or his Russian wife, and Ugrumov declined. The following year he took Russian nationality. He now lives in Italy. The life of Ugrumov's Soviet Union team-mate Andrei Tchmil, the son of an operatic soprano from Odessa, poses an even greater challenge to any simple identity of athlete with nation. Born to a Ukrainian mother and a Russian father in Khabarovsk, a remote settlement lost in the vastness of the USSR, he lived in Crimea and Moldova, before moving west to Rimini, north to Belgium (Charleroi, then Waregem), south to France (Roubaix), then back to Italy. He represented the Soviet Union until 1992, then Moldova. In 1995, after the Moldovan Cycling Federation had asked Tchmil to pay several thousand dollars for his racing licence, he moved to Kiev in the Ukraine, and represented the nation of his mother tongue until 1997, when he took a Belgian racing licence.

Despite these complications, the nation is a convenient rubric, and international bodies compile detailed league tables, arranging the world's nations in order according to everything from availability of information technology to provision of clean water. Yet one of the most influential indicators affecting popular conceptions of global development must be sporting success – a window on the world that, although imperfect, may have some basis in reality. There may be an investment threshold at which a nation's success in sport depends more on the efficiency and resources of the national sports system than on the effort of individual athletes. When that threshold is reached, sport becomes a system, first national, then global, and loses all pretence of being apolitical in the battle of representations that, like Sunset Boulevard, reinvents history to suit its economic, political, ideological needs.

These tables and classifications, however, may hold the key to understanding why sport is pleasurable, too. Could it be that, unable to make sense of ourselves, we look for understanding outside, and those classifications and league tables offer a model for knowing our place in the universe? And that we ride, or write, or do what we do, partly in order to be judged (although not necessarily by those who do judge us, or according to their criteria)? It is precisely this judgement that the domestique, like us, cannot know, is forbidden from knowing – which is why he consoles himself with the thought, 'One day, my turn will come,' and we follow. For he is an image of the variation in individual human capacities, illustrating what we have always known: that there are individuals who, even given the same input and the same stimuli as everyone else, produce an incomparably superior output. Some see with greater understanding than us and formulate what they see with greater clarity and evocation than we ever could. Others instantly grasp relations between complex numbers where we gaze blankly, like idiots. Still others climb mountain passes so fast that, when we try to follow, we soon find ourselves drowning in the atmosphere. They shatter our ideal of equal opportunities: the genius, in whatever field, *should* have greater opportunity than his inferiors. As the domestiques consume their final drops of energy before peeling away and disappearing into oblivion, the altruism they exhibit captures, perhaps, the inherent lack of fulfilment we all experience – for there must be waste even in a fortunate life, which worldly reform could prevent only by degree. Perhaps this is the truth with which cycling tantalises us: that we can sometimes see more clearly through half-closed eyes, read history books for what they suppress, refuse to discriminate between core and peripheral vision and derive strange pleasure from unexpectedly discovering – in reflections we have despised, knowledge we have repressed, feelings we have scorned – visions and values that enhance our lives.

Optimism, of course, shaped the age that bore this unusual sport – an age that fervently believed that the speed and vitality exemplified in the racing cyclist would, with advances in schooling and scientific knowledge, power humanity towards ceaseless improvements in private and public ethics, political tolerance and global understanding. The intervening century has seen much of that buoyancy betrayed. The Tour has seen education, intellect and technology proven compatible with cruelty and indifference, and passed into a time when weapons flow freely to each new holocaust, and in which we squander what is left of nature's resources and live unconcerned by the juxtaposition of western overabundance and the destitution that afflicts three-fifths of mankind. No longer content with faster, higher, stronger, we crave the fastest, highest and strongest, whatever the human cost.

Epilogue

The day after Lance Armstrong's extraordinary victory at Luz-Ardiden, another American, thirty-two-year-old Tyler Hamilton, spent almost the entire day on the attack and won the final Pyrenean stage. On the final straight he turned around to point at his team director, 1996 Tour winner Bjarne Riis, and shook his hand through the car window. His victory, with a one-minute fifty-five-second advantage over the peloton, was even more astonishing in that Hamilton had broken his collarbone in two places in the mass fall at the end of stage one at Meaux, near Paris. Hamilton climbed from seventh to sixth in GC. The top of the classification remained unchanged, with Armstrong one minute seven seconds ahead of Ullrich and two minutes forty-five seconds ahead of Vinokourov; they came to the finish line with the field. At the finish Hamilton and Armstrong fell into each other's arms. Hamilton had been Armstrong's domestique in two of his Tour successes.

Then the peloton sped north for two days, covering the flatlands that led to Pornic on the Atlantic coast, and the starting line for the final time trial. Fifty kilometres into stage eighteen, Jan Ullrich surged unexpectedly before the intermediate sprint at Montendre. Armstrong followed, but the German won a two-second bonus over his rival. He would start the final time trial with sixty-five seconds to make up.

The previous evening, I asked Armstrong if he was confident he could resist Ullrich's challenge. Lance looked me in the eye and asked: 'What does history say?' The history to which he was referring was recent: Armstrong had never lost the final time trial in a Tour de France. But history, as usual, went both ways. In 1968, Jan Janssen stole the yellow jersey in the final time trial. In 1989, Greg Lemond did the same. Now, on 26 July 2004, pouring rain made the roads treacherous. In such conditions, anything could happen. 'That morning,' remembers Victor Hugo Peña, 'Lance said, "I've lost one time trial to Ullrich. I'm not going to lose another."'

Ullrich started at incredible speed, gaining six seconds in the first two kilometres, putting the pressure on Armstrong. But Armstrong had already made up the lost time when the German fell heavily and skidded across the asphalt on the run in to the finish at Nantes. Millar won the stage, ahead of Hamilton, who leapfrogged the Basques into fourth place overall. Armstrong was able to coast safely to the finish, where he took third place in the stage, with Ullrich just behind. On the finish line, secure of his yellow jersey and his place in history, Lance Armstrong allowed himself to clench his fist in triumph. That Victor Hugo Peña finished seventh, just one minute behind Millar, was irrelevant to the race result.

The final stage ended with twelve ritual ascents of the Champs-Élysées. As the file of riders crossed the finish line for the last time, an almost imperceptible gap opened behind the eighty-fifth rider. The following fifty-two riders were attributed a time fifteen seconds slower than the first group. By finishing in the front peloton, Jan Ullrich moved to within sixty-one seconds of his vanquisher. It might as well have been eternity. Victor Hugo crossed the line with Pavel Padrnos. Siamese twins.

All nine US Postal riders completed the Tour. Beltrán and Rubiera, Armstrong's mountain lieutenants, were fourteenth and nineteenth in GC. Heras was thirty-fourth, having lost time due to illness. Hincapie and Landis, paid to lead through the foothills, were forty-seventh and seventy-seventh. Ekimov, Peña and Padrnos, the workers on the flat, finished seventy-sixth, eighty-eighth and one hundred and second. These positions were pure functions of their team roles, not reflections of their talent.

The evening ended with parties of celebration or commiseration. Armstrong and his team-mates were overjoyed. Victor Hugo Peña recalls: 'On the last day of the Tour I said to Lance, *I don't know how happy you are today, but I think my happiness is greater than yours, working for you, working for this team*. Money can't buy the happiness I have. I'm lucky. I was chosen to be part of this United Nations of cycling: a team that takes a rider from each country, and from Colombia, it took me.'

But Victor Hugo's joy, straightforward at the time, was complicated by hindsight:

Look at Tyler Hamilton. In the spring, he won a prestigious one-day classic, the Liège–Bastogne–Liège, and a high-profile one-week stage race, the Tour of Romandie, around French-speaking Switzerland. Without his broken collarbone, some think he might have challenged Armstrong. But more than Hamilton, I think of his director, Bjarne Riis. I once read that Riis learned everything he knew – professionalism, discipline, everything – from Laurent Fignon [Tour de France champion in 1983 and 1984]. Riis was Fignon's domestique, but afterwards he finished in the top ten, then fifth, then third, and then he won. Obviously, you have to be hard, strong. But one day I want to come to compete for the Tour, to show that I can be among the leaders.

The Armstrong cycle will end sooner or later, perhaps at the end of 2004. There won't be a rider like Armstrong around, so I hope I'll have some freedom. Although Lance is so good perhaps he'll want to win seven Tours, or nine ... Last year, after he'd won the Tour, he was asked, 'Do you want to win five?' And he said, 'Yes, but why not six, and seven?' He was joking, although at night, in the silence, he must think, 'I can win six, or seven.' Sooner or later, though, he'll stop. And when he does, I hope I'll have a chance to win the Tour de France.

I too hope my friend will one day get his chance. Perhaps – probably – he won't win the Tour. Perhaps he'll finish third, or fifth or eighth. All that matters is that he will have had his chance. Whether he does or not, the Tour de France will carry on, exercising its peculiar capacity for absorbing the ambitions and frustrations of a nation's demography, big questions and others seen only side on, and releasing them year after year as a collective fantasy. And where other sports, packaged into polished wholes, offer comfort and illusion, cycling – this sport of frayed edges and awkward silences – will continue to serve us with the truths we resist, the reflections we blink at, the lessons we refuse to learn, expressed over and again in a rush of men trying to win a bicycle race.

Glossary

bidon and **musette** (both *French*) The bidon is a plastic bottle for carrying water and sports drinks. The musette is a cotton bag with a shoulder strap filled with food and distributed by *soigneurs* (see below) at designated feed zones, or used by small boys to lasso handlebars. At the Tour de France, musettes and 500 ml bidons are supplied by the race organisers. The use of unofficial musettes and bidons is strictly prohibited at the Tour.

directeur sportif (*French*) Responsible before the sport's governing bodies for team organisation and conduct, the directeur sportif (or DS) recruits riders, dictates their race programmes, provides training routines and, during races, directs team strategy from the wheel of a team car. Since the early 1990s, DSs have been able to communicate with their riders via lightweight two-way radios. At the Tour, each team nominates a directeur sportif and an assistant directeur sportif. They ride in two race vehicles provided to each team by the Tour organisation.

domestique (*French*) A rider whose task is to work in order to further his team leader's prospects of victory. The original meaning of domestique was a member of the royal court; by extension, it came to mean a domestic servant.

dossard (*French*) The race number worn on the rider's back. Article Two of the Tour de France Regulations stipulates: 'Riders ... shall wear two dossards (in small format) over the hips, one to the left and one to the right. During time trial events, one large-format dossard shall be affixed in the centre of the back.' On abandoning the race, riders are stripped of a dossard – an act of public humiliation, according to the etiquette of the sport.

echelon (*French*) A formation in which riders fan across the road behind the front rider to get maximum draft in a crosswind.

entraîneur (*French*) In the early history of cycling, an assistant (or one of a number of assistants) who rode ahead of the cyclist on a bicycle, tandem, triplet, quadruplet, motorbike or automobile, to provide a slipstream.

gruppetto (*Italian*) A large compact group of cyclists far behind the leaders, interested only in crossing the finish line within the time limit for the day, calculated as a percentage of the stage winner's average speed according to the type of stage and difficulties involved.

musette (*French*) see **bidon**

peloton (*French*) A large compact group of cyclists. There may be one or more pelotons at any given moment. Literally, a peloton is a ball of wool or string. The word was first used figuratively in a military sense to describe a group of soldiers (the English word platoon derives from French *peloton*).

rouleur (*French*) A cyclist capable of riding in the lead position on flat or rolling stages for long periods.

routier (*French*) A road-racer (as opposed to a **pistard** or track specialist).

soigneur (*French*) Known in the Regulations of cycling's governing body as a Paramedical Assistant, the soigneur (literally, carer) is principally a masseur, although he is also expected to prepare riders'

musettes (see **bidon**, above), deliver their luggage to the hotel, take responsibility for team laundry, drive anywhere at any time of day or night, and act as bodyguard when necessary.

tempo (*Italian*) A comfortable pace.

touriste-routier (*French*) From 1923 to 1931, and again in 1935 and 1936, riders who participated in the Tour de France as individuals, paying their own expenses (in 1923, 'touristes-routiers' paid FF125 for the transport of their clothes by Tour vehicles).

Appendix

It is possible to compile a table of the most successful nations (see below). The most important indicator of success is the number of overall Tour wins. Riders from eleven nations have achieved overall victory, and those nations should fill the top eleven positions in the table, according to the number of overall victories they have achieved: France (thirty-six wins), Belgium (eighteen), Italy (nine), Spain (eight) and USA (eight), Luxembourg (four), Netherlands (two), Switzerland (two), Germany (one), Ireland (one) and Denmark (one). Ambiguities still remaining after total overall wins have been taken into account – between Spain and the USA, between Germany, Ireland and Denmark, and between the remaining thirty-nine nations who have no overall wins – have to be resolved using other criteria.

My table treats the mountains category, the points competition and a top-three podium finish as equal achievements, on the basis that they are equally common, followed, in the scale of achievement, by the race lead. Since there are fewer race leaders than stage winners, and since the race leader has since 1919 worn the distinctive yellow jersey for the duration of his leadership, with its special charge of prestige, I have made the race lead superior to a stage win. As a team's nationality is given only by that of the majority of its riders, I have given it less weight in a table intended to compare the achievements of nationalities at the Tour. And the Best Young Rider category, the only annual title disputed by a restricted number of participants, is the smallest value of the entire palette. Once all these criteria have been applied, nations still on an equal standing can be sorted on a proportional basis: those nationalities who have had the fewest participations, and therefore the fewest opportunities, stand above those who have had more opportunities yet have achieved the same success, or lack of it.

Internationalisation of participants and success
(Tour de France 1903–2003)

[Year of first (total)]	Participations	BYR title	Team title	Stage wins
1 France	1903 (4690)	1979 (5)	1930 (30)	1903 (659)
2 Belgium	1903 (1934)		1931 (11)	1909 (457)
3 Italy	1903 (1494)	1975 (4)	1932 (7)	1910 (247)
4 Spain	1910 (1123)	1976 (4)	1974 (8)	1929 (100)
5 USA	1981 (115)	1984 (2)		1985 (27)
6 Luxembourg	1906 (150)			1908 (61)
7 Netherlands	1936 (729)	1978 (5)	1953 (5)	1936 (167)
8 Switzerland	1903 (440)		1954 (1)	1903 (49)
9 Germany*	1903 (339)	1977 (4)	1997 (1)	1931 (54)
10 Ireland	1956 (42)			1963 (10)
11 Denmark	1913 (115)		2003 (1)	1970 (13)
12 Colombia	1975 (180)	1985 (2)		1984 (12)
13 Australia	1914 (71)	1982 (1)		1982 (10)
14 Portugal	1956 (50)			1969 (7)
15 Uzbekistan	1992 (6)			1992 (6)
16 Austria	1931 (41)			1931 (3)
17 Poland	1947 (25)			1993 (1)
18 Great Britain	1937 (136)			1958 (24)
19 USSR	1990 (16)			1990 (4)
20 Latvia	1994 (12)			1994 (2)
21 Kazakhstan	1993 (13)			2003 (1)
22 Sweden	1960 (16)			1998 (1)
23 Lithuania	1992 (8)			
24 Russia	1992 (51)	2003 (1)		1992 (7)
25 Estonia	1993 (10)			1999 (3)
26 Canada	1984 (14)			1988 (1)
27 Mexico	1986 (9)	1987 (1)		1989 (2)

* East and West

Race lead	KoM title	Points title	Top 3 finishes	Overall wins
1903 (706)	1934 (18)	1957 (9)	1903 (96)	1903 (36)
1904 (473)	1935 (11)	1955 (18)	1904 (50)	1912 (18)
1912 (188)	1938 (12)	1968 (1)	1923 (37)	1924 (9)
1955 (115)	1933 (15)		1952 (22)	1959 (8)
1986 (81)			1984 (11)	1986 (8)
1909 (80)	1955 (2)		1908 (10)	1909 (4)
1951 (74)	1988 (2)	1964 (4)	1966 (15)	1968 (2)
1904 (45)	1993 (1)	1953 (2)	1937 (9)	1950 (2)
1932 (75)		1962 (8)	1932 (6)	1997 (1)
1963 (5)		1982 (4)	1985 (2)	1987 (1)
1983 (34)			1995 (2)	1996 (1)
2003 (3)	1985 (2)		1988 (1)	
1981 (23)		2002 (2)		
1989 (4)			1978 (2)	
		1992 (2)		
1931 (1)			1957 (1)	
1987 (2)			1993 (1)	
1962 (7)	1984 (1)			
		1991 (1)		
			1994 (1)	
			2003 (1)	
			1970 (1)	
			2002 (1)	
1996 (2)				
1999 (6)				
1986 (15)				

	Participations	BYR title	Team title	Stage wins (total)
28 Czech Rep.	1997 (11)			1998 (2)
29 Norway	1975 (28)			1987 (2)
30 Slovakia	1993 (2)			1994 (1)
31 Brazil	1986 (4)			1991 (1)
32 Morocco	1949 (5)			1950 (1)
33 Ukraine	1993 (12)			1995 (1)
34 Algeria	1910 (29)			1950 (1)
35 New Zealand	1928 (11)			
36 Yugoslavia	1936 (8)			
37 Slovenia	1995 (6)			
38 Venezuela	1993 (5)			
39 Monte Carlo	1921 (4)			
40 Moldova	1994 (4)			
41 Romania	1936 (4)			
42 Japan	1926 (3)			
43 South Africa	2001 (3)			
44 Czechoslovakia	1987 (3)			
45 Saarland	1957 (3)			
46 Finland	1997 (2)			
47 Hungary	2002 (2)			
48 Tunisia	1913 (2)			
49 Croatia	2003 (1)			
50 Liechtenstein	1954 (1)			

Race lead	KoM title	Points title	Top 3 finishes	Overall wins

Acknowledgements

Victor Hugo Peña agreed to contribute to this book in November 2002, when the events of the year to come – the armed robbery at his home in Colombia, nearly missing the Tour as a result, then riding the Centenary Tour on a tourist visa (a modern *touriste-routier*!), becoming the first Colombian to wear the yellow jersey before witnessing this remarkable event unfold – lay behind the corner of time. With charm, humour and rigour, Victor Hugo shaped this book and channelled my thinking with wisdom and moderation. I offer him my gratitude.

Nic Cheetham gave so generously of his time, energy and expertise that, like Victor Hugo, he should consider this book partly his own. Edgar Medellín allowed me to share in his understanding and restraint. David Luxton first asked me to make a proposal for this series. Richard Milner, Mark Rusher and Francine Brody oversaw this book from start to finish. Peter Keen, Chester 'Chet' Kyle and Asker Jeukendrup kindly provided me with reading lists. Ralph Beneke of the University of Essex has adapted parts of chapter three as the basis for a multi-disciplined attempt to model the behaviour of pelotons. John Rendell had the generosity and stamina to scrutinise the entire first draft, and made numerous helpful suggestions. Anna Rendell-Knights and Bryans Knights were patient listeners.

Lance Armstrong and Johan Bruyneel have been unfailingly kind and accessible to my questioning in media scrums at the Tour and the calmer surroundings of hotels all over Europe. I thank them especially for charitably offering coherent responses to my sometimes less than coherent questions at the more frenzied moments of the Tour. US Postal press officer Jogi Müller has always been extremely helpful, as were Victor Hugo's neighbours in and around Javia: Matt White, Claus Moller and Julian Dean.

I also gratefully acknowledge conversations with the following: Manolo Sáiz; Fulvio Acquati; Santiago Botero and family; Iván Parra and family; Gianni Savio; Andrei Tchmil; Piotr Ugrumov; Benjamin Laverde; Alfredo Castro; Hector Urrego; Pablo Arbeláez; Andrew Simms; Ken McGill; Javier García Sánchez. I thank VTV Ltd and Steve Docherty for inviting me to be part of their production team at the Tour de France, and indirectly making this book possible. Thanks are also due to my wonderful wife, Viviana.

I also wish to acknowledge a longstanding personal debt to two appreciated friends and mentors: Dr Riccardo Steiner and Gary Imlach.

Index